THE SLANGMAN GUIDE TO

STREET SPEAK 1

THE COMPLETE COURSE IN AMERICAN SLANG & IDIOMS

Front cover:

tie the knot (to) *exp.* to get married.

SLANGMAN DAVID BURKE

A SPECIAL THANKS

This book is based on the *STREET TALK Student Book* by David Burke and David Harrington. A very special thanks goes to David Harrington, the author of *"Speaking of Speech," "Discover Debate," Getting Ready for Speech," "Listen Kids," "Hi Performance,"* and *"What's in the Cards?"* His help in paving the way for a new exciting look for the series is highly appreciated. I am grateful for his sense of cleverness, endless imagination and creativity. I admire his sense of humor and style.

Meet
"Slangman" David Burke

Being brought up in a multi-lingual household, David Burke used his language skills as a tour guide at Universal Studios in Hollywood, California, giving tours in English, French, Italian, and sign language.

His love of language inspired him to delve into the intricacies of words and led him to become a prominent author of more than 60 books on understanding slang and idioms in different languages, as well as books that teach kids foreign languages through fairy tales.

His materials on slang and idioms are currently used as course curriculum by Berlitz International, UCLA, Harvard University, NYU and Hewlett Packard, and even by the writers of *The Simpsons* to give Bart his coolness.

Having been trained since the age of four as a classical pianist (along with the cello, recorder, classical guitar, harp, organ, and harpsichord), his prior career was as a composer for a variety of television shows produced by Grant Tinker.

David was then asked to join the Los Angeles Olympic Organizing Committee as their in-house composer for all their documentaries, commercials, and public service announcements during which he worked with Phyllis Diller, Bob Hope, and Lou Rawls.

In 1986, David founded Slangman, Inc. (including Slangman Publishing and Slangman Kids), a publishing company specializing in materials that teach children foreign languages, as well as products teaching teens and adults slang and idioms in a variety of languages.

In 1999, David became known as *"Slangman"* to 90 million listeners in 120 countries due to his regular 5-year segment on *Voice of America's "Coast to Coast."*

David has appeared on more than 250 national and international radio and television programs helping parents to understand their teens. David was also a commentator during several Academy Awards broadcasts for the BBC's *Five Live* (a program broadcasting to 7 million people throughout the United Kingdom) to speak about slang used in American movies and TV shows.

Currently, David has pooled all his talents together to create *HEY WORDY!*, a children's TV show, which introduces children ages 3+ to the world of foreign languages and cultures in an environment of music, puppetry, animation, and magic. *HEY WORDY!* airs in 176 countries. Visit www.heywordy.com for more information.

Book Design and Production: Slangman Publishing
Design (Logo/Web): Jennifer Reese
Editor: Julie Bobrick
Illustrator – Outside cover & contributing artist: Ty Semaka
Icon Design: Sharon Kim
Contributing artist: Ty Semaka

Copyright © 2000, 2005, 2014 by David Burke
Published by Slangman Publishing, Los Angeles, CA
Fax: 1-413-647-1589
Email: info@slangman.com
Website: www.slangman.com

The Slangman Guide to Street Speak 1:
ISBN: 1891888080
ISBN13: 9781891888083

Printed in the United States of America

LEGEND

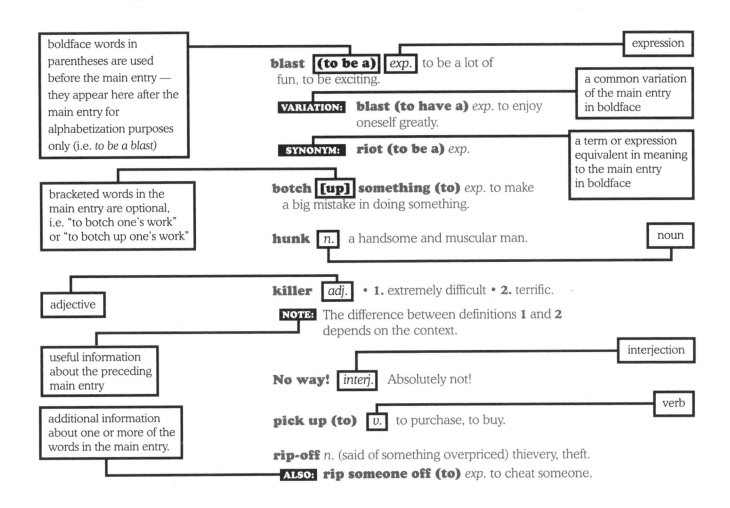

boldface words in parentheses are used before the main entry — they appear here after the main entry for alphabetization purposes only (i.e. *to be a blast*)

blast **(to be a)** *exp.* to be a lot of fun, to be exciting.

expression

VARIATION: **blast (to have a)** *exp.* to enjoy oneself greatly.

a common variation of the main entry in boldface

SYNONYM: **riot (to be a)** *exp.*

a term or expression equivalent in meaning to the main entry in boldface

bracketed words in the main entry are optional, i.e. "to botch one's work" or "to botch up one's work"

botch **[up]** **something (to)** *exp.* to make a big mistake in doing something.

hunk *n.* a handsome and muscular man.

noun

adjective

killer *adj.* • **1.** extremely difficult • **2.** terrific.

NOTE: The difference between definitions **1** and **2** depends on the context.

useful information about the preceding main entry

interjection

No way! *interj.* Absolutely not!

verb

additional information about one or more of the words in the main entry.

pick up (to) *v.* to purchase, to buy.

rip-off *n.* (said of something overpriced) thievery, theft.
ALSO: **rip someone off (to)** *exp.* to cheat someone.

EXPLANATION OF ICONS

These exercises reinforce visual recognition of the slang terms and idioms presented throughout this book.

These exercises include fill-ins, crossword puzzles, word matches and many other fun word games to help you use the new terms in context.

One of the most important parts of any language is to be able to understand what you hear. These exercises can all be found on the audio program. *(See coupon on back page for details)*

These oral exercises are designed to help you to begin speaking and thinking like a native.

TABLE OF CONTENTS

LESSON TITLE	WORDS PRESENTED

ACTIVITIES

LET'S WARM UP!
`READING`

LET'S TALK!
`LISTENING/SPEAKING`
A. Dialogue (*Slang & Idioms*)
B. Dialogue (*Translated*)
C. Dialogue (*in "Real Speak"*)
`KEY TO "REAL SPEAK"`
Did You = Did 'Ja

LET'S USE "REAL SPEAK!"
`READING`
A. Wha'did they say?
`SPEAKING`
B. Did'ja or Didn'chu?

LET'S PRACTICE!
`READING`
A. Context Exercise
`READING`
B. Choose the Right Word
`WRITING`
C. Complete the Phrase
`SPEAKING`
D. Is it "Yes" or is it "No"?

LET'S WARM UP!
`READING`

LET'S TALK!
`LISTENING/SPEAKING`
A. Dialogue (*Slang & Idioms*)
B. Dialogue (*Translated*)
C. Dialogue (*in "Real Speak"*)
`KEY TO "REAL SPEAK"`
"T" = "D" • ...ED = 'D, 'T, or 'ID?

LET'S USE "REAL SPEAK!"
`SPEAKING`
A. "T" Pronounced Like "D"

LET'S PRACTICE!
`WRITING`
A. TV Commercial
`WRITING`
B. You're the Author
`READING`
C. True or False
`READING`
D. Crossword Puzzle

LET'S WARM UP!
`READING`

LET'S TALK!
`LISTENING/SPEAKING`
A. Dialogue (*Slang & Idioms*)
B. Dialogue (*Translated*)
C. Dialogue (*in "Real Speak"*)
`KEY TO "REAL SPEAK"`
Must Have = Must'a • Would'a, Should'a, Could'a

LET'S USE "REAL SPEAK!"
`WRITING`
A. Should'a, Could'a
   Would'a, Must'a

LET'S PRACTICE!
`WRITING`
A. I Know the Answer, But
   What's the Question?
`READING`
B. Find Your Perfect Match
`SPEAKING`
C. Imagine That...

LET'S WARM UP!
`READING`

LET'S TALK!
`LISTENING/SPEAKING`
A. Dialogue (*Slang & Idioms*)
B. Dialogue (*Translated*)
C. Dialogue (*in "Real Speak"*)
`KEY TO "REAL SPEAK"`
And = 'N • In = 'N

LET'S USE "REAL SPEAK!"
`SPEAKING`
A. Put the Pairs Back Together

LET'S PRACTICE!
`WRITING`
A. Find the Missing Words
`READING`
B. Match the Sentences

LET'S WARM UP!
`READING`

LET'S TALK!
`LISTENING/SPEAKING`
A. Dialogue (*Slang & Idioms*)
B. Dialogue (*Translated*)
C. Dialogue (*in "Real Speak"*)
`KEY TO "REAL SPEAK"`
To = Ta or Da

LET'S USE "REAL SPEAK!"
`WRITING`
A. "Across" Word Puzzle
`SPEAKING`
B. "Ta Be" or not "Ta Be"

LET'S PRACTICE!
`WRITING`
A. Complete the Fairy Tale
`READING`
B. Context Exercise
`WRITING`
C. Complete the Phrase

TABLE OF CONTENTS (CONTINUED)

ACTIVITIES

LET'S WARM UP!
`READING`

LET'S TALK!
`LISTENING/SPEAKING`
A. Dialogue (*Slang & Idioms*)
B. Dialogue (*Translated*)
C. Dialogue (*in "Real Speak"*)
`KEY TO "REAL SPEAK"`
Going To = Gonna

LET'S USE "REAL SPEAK!"
`SPEAKING`
A. Now You're Gonna Do
a "Gonna" Exercise
`READING`
B. Is it *Gonna* or *Going to*?

LET'S PRACTICE!
`READING`
A. Choose the Right Word
`WRITING`
B. Crossword Puzzle
`READING`
C. Match the Column

LET'S WARM UP!
`READING`

LET'S TALK!
`LISTENING/SPEAKING`
A. Dialogue (*Slang & Idioms*)
B. Dialogue (*Translated*)
C. Dialogue (*in "Real Speak"*)
`KEY TO "REAL SPEAK"`
Want To = Wanna

LET'S USE "REAL SPEAK!"
`SPEAKING`
A. Wanna or Wansta

LET'S PRACTICE!
`READING`
A. Correct or Incorrect
`WRITING`
B. Blank-Blank
`READING`
C. True or False

LET'S WARM UP!
`READING`

LET'S TALK!
`LISTENING/SPEAKING`
A. Dialogue (*Slang & Idioms*)
B. Dialogue (*Translated*)
C. Dialogue (*in "Real Speak"*)
`KEY TO "REAL SPEAK"`
He='E • Him='Im • His='Is • Her='Er • Them = 'Em

LET'S USE "REAL SPEAK!"
`WRITING`
A. Should'a, Could'a
Would'a, Must'a
`SPEAKING & WRITING`
A. Change 'Em to Real Speak

LET'S PRACTICE!
`READING`
A. Truth or Lie
`WRITING`
B. Find the Definition
`WRITING`
C. Find-The-Word Grid

LET'S WARM UP!
`READING`

LET'S TALK!
`LISTENING/SPEAKING`
A. Dialogue (*Slang & Idioms*)
B. Dialogue (*Translated*)
C. Dialogue (*in "Real Speak"*)
`KEY TO "REAL SPEAK"`
You=Ya • Your=Yer • You're=Yer • Yours=Yers

LET'S USE "REAL SPEAK!"
`WRITING`
A. Unscramble

LET'S PRACTICE!
`WRITING`
A. Unfinished Conversation
`READING`
B. Choose the Right Word
`WRITING`
C. Complete the Story

LET'S WARM UP!
`READING`

LET'S TALK!
`LISTENING/SPEAKING`
A. Dialogue (*Slang & Idioms*)
B. Dialogue (*Translated*)
C. Dialogue (*in "Real Speak"*)
`KEY TO "REAL SPEAK"`
Have To = Hafta • Has To = Hasta

LET'S USE "REAL SPEAK!"
`SPEAKING & WRITING`
A. Now You Hafta Do a
"Hafta" Exercise

LET'S PRACTICE!
`WRITING`
A. Create Your Own Story
(*Part 1*)
`SPEAKING`
B. Create Your Own Story
(*Part 2*)
`READING`
C. What Would You Do If
Someone Said...?

AT THE PARTY!

"I'm having a blast!"

LET'S WARM UP!

MATCH THE PICTURES *(Answers on p. 131)*

As a fun way to get started, see if you can guess the meaning of the new slang words and expressions on the opposite page by using the pictures below and following the context of the sentences.

READING

1. Don't get so upset! **Get a grip**!
   "*Get a grip*" means: . . . . ❑ Leave me alone . . . . ❑ Get control of your emotions

2. What a great party! I'm **having a blast**!
   "*having a blast*" means: . . . . . . ❑ terribly bored . . . . ❑ having a great time

3. Rob seems a little upset. **What's up with** him?
   "*What's up with him*" means: . . . . ❑ What's wrong with him?. . . . ❑ What's he wearing?

4. That's not his real hair. I think it's a **rug**.
   "*I think it's a rug*" means: . . . . . . ❑ I think it's a hairpiece . . . . . ❑ I think it's a shirt

5. That story can't be true. You're **putting me on**.
   "*You're putting me on*" means: . . . ❑ You're disagreeing with me. . ❑ You're kidding me

6. **Get a load of** that dress. Isn't it ugly?
   "*Get a load of that dress*" means: . . ❑ Look at that dress . . . . . . ❑ Buy that dress

7. David exercises a lot. He's a **hunk**.
   "*He's a hunk*" means: . . . . ❑ He's an idiot . . . . ❑ He's a muscular man

8. You drove down that one-way street against traffic?! **No way**!
   "*No way!*" means: . . . . ❑ That's wonderful! . . . . . . ❑ That's impossible!

9. Why do you keep criticizing me?! **Get off my case**!
   "*Get off my case*" means: . . . . . . ❑ Go on a trip! . . . . ❑ Stop nagging me!

10. I'm not inviting Diane to my party. I **can't stand** her.
    "*I can't stand her*" means: . . . . . . ❑ I really like her . . . . ❑ I can't tolerate her

LET'S TALK!

A. DIALOGUE USING SLANG & IDIOMS

The words introduced on the first two pages are used in the following dialogue and illustrated in the long picture above. Can you understand the conversation and find the illustration that corresponds to the slang? *Note:* The translation of the words in boldface is on the right-hand page.

SPEAKING   LISTENING

CD-A: TRACK 2

Debbie and Becky are attending a party.

Debbie: I don't know why I let you convince me to come here. I hate parties.

Becky: Would you **get a grip**? This is going to be a **blast**!

Debbie: Oh, no. Look who just walked in. Sheila Hampton. I **can't stand** her. She always **gets on my case** because she doesn't like the way I dress.

Becky: What?! Did you **get a load of** that tiny dress she's wearing? Her belt's so tight it looks like she's being cut in half! Hey, isn't that Ernie Milton she's with?

Debbie: Yeah, you're right. He's gained so much weight! And **what's up with** his hair?

Becky: What hair? I don't know what you think, but I think it's a **rug**.

Debbie: **No way**! You're **putting me on**! He was such a **hunk**! He's changed so much in ten years!

Becky: I remember. I wonder what happened to him. Uh oh. I think Sheila's waving at us. They're both coming this way!

Debbie: Oh, no. Run!

B. DIALOGUE TRANSLATED INTO STANDARD ENGLISH

LET'S SEE HOW MUCH YOU REMEMBER!
Just for fun, bounce around in random order to the words and expressions in boldface below. See if you can remember their slang equivalents without looking at the left-hand page!

Debbie and Becky are attending a party.

Debbie: I don't know why I let you convince me to come here. I hate parties.

Becky: Would you **get control of your emotions**? This is going to be a **great time**!

Debbie: Oh, no. Look who just walked in. Sheila Hampton. I can't **tolerate** her. She always **criticizes me** because she doesn't like the way I dress.

Becky: What?! Did you **take a good look at** that tiny dress she's wearing? Her belt's so tight it looks like she's being cut in half! Hey, isn't that Ernie Milton she's with?

Debbie: Yeah, you're right. He's gained so much weight! And **what's wrong with** his hair?

Becky: What hair? I don't know what you think, but I think it's a **hairpiece**.

Debbie: **That's impossible! You're kidding me**! He was such a **muscular and handsome guy**! He's changed so much in ten years!

Becky: I remember. I wonder what happened to him. Uh oh. I think Sheila's waving at us. They're both coming this way!

Debbie: Oh, no. Run!

C. DIALOGUE USING "REAL SPEAK"

The dialogue below demonstrates how the slang conversation on the previous page would *really* be spoken by native speakers!

CD-A: TRACK 2

Debbie 'n Becky'er attending a pardy.

Debbie: I dunno why I letchu convince me da come here. I hate pardies.

Becky: Would'ja **ged a grip**? This'ez gonna be a **blast**!

Debbie: Oh, no. Look 'oo jus' walked in. Sheila Hampton. I **can't stand** 'er. She always **gets on my case** 'cuz she doesn' like the way I dress.

Becky: What?! Did'ja **ged a load of** that tiny dress she's wearing? Her belt's so tide it looks like she's being cud 'n half! Hey, isn't that Ernie Milton she's with?

Debbie: Yeah, yer right. He's gained so much weight! An' **what's up with** 'is hair?

Becky: What hair? I dunno whatchu think, bud I think it's a **rug**.

Debbie: **No way**! Yer **pudding me on**! He was such a **hunk**! He's changed so much 'n ten years!

Becky: I remember. I wonder what happened ta him. Uh oh. I think Sheila's waving ad us. They're both coming this way!

Debbie: Oh, no. Run!

KEY TO "REAL SPEAK"
DID YOU = DID'JA

In the above dialogue using "real speak," the phrase "Did you hear" became **Did'ja** hear." In everyday pronunciation, the personal pronoun "you" can take on some popular forms as seen below:

RULES

D + Y = J

When a word ending in "d" is followed by a word beginning with "y," the "y" takes the sound of "j."

did you = **did'ju** or **did'ja**
would you = **would'ju** or **would'ja**

T + Y = CH

When a word ending in "t" is followed by a word beginning with "y," the "y" takes the sound of "ch."

let you = **let'chu** or **let'cha**
what you = **what'chu** or **what'cha**

HOW DOES IT WORK?

Did you eat yet?

Did **y**ou eat **y**et?
↓   ↓
Did **j**ou eat **ch**et?

In this sentence, the "y" in "you" follows a "d" and takes the sound of "**j**." The "y" in "yet" follows a "t" and takes the sound of "**ch**."

Did **j**ou eat **ch**et?
↓
Did **j**uh eat **ch**et?

The unstressed vowel combination "*ou*" in "*you*" is commonly pronounced **uh** (often seen written as "**a**"). Therefore, "*you*" becomes **ya** or, in this case, **ja** since the letter "y" is preceded by a "d."

Did'**ja** eat'**ch**et?

BUT!

When "you" **is** stressed (meaning that the voice goes up), it is pronounced "**ju**":

*No. Did you? = No. Did'**ju***

Also, when "you" is preceded by "did" and is part of a compound subject, it is pronounced "**ju**":

*Did <u>you</u> and <u>Nancy</u> have fun at the party? = Did'**ju** and Nancy have fun at the party?*

LET'S USE "REAL SPEAK!"

CD-A: TRACK 3

A. WHA'DID THEY SAY? *(Answers on p. 131)*

Match the sentence in "real speak" with the standard English translation by checking the appropriate box.

1. **What did'ja do?**
   - ☐ a. What do you do?
   - ☐ b. What did you do?

2. **I want'cha to leave.**
   - ☐ a. I want you to leave.
   - ☐ b. I want to chew a leaf.

3. **Didn'cha finish your homework? Not'chet.**
   - ☐ a. Didn't you finish your homework? Not yet.
   - ☐ b. Did you finish your homework? Not yet.

4. **Why don'cha get'cher car fixed?**
   - ☐ a. Why don't you get your car fixed?
   - ☐ b. Why don't you get her car fixed?

5. **Is that'cher book?**
   - ☐ a. Is that your book?
   - ☐ b. Is that chair broke?

6. **Did'ja eat'chet? No, did'ju?**
   - ☐ a. Did you eat yet? No, did you?
   - ☐ b. Did you cheat, Chet? No, did you?

CD-A: TRACK 4

B. DID'JA OR DIDN'CHU?

Read the question or statement out loud from Column 1 with the response from Column 2. Then start again using the short version response from Column 3.

COLUMN 1	COLUMN 2	COLUMN 3 *(short version)*
*Did'**ja** go?*	*No. Did'**JU** go?* **OR**	*No. Did'**JU**?*
*I thought'**cha** left yesterday.*	*Really? I thought'**CHU** left yesterday!* **OR**	*Really? I thought'**CHU** did!*
*Did'**ja** finish your homework?*	*Yeah. Did'**JU** finish your homework?* **OR**	*Yeah. Did'**JU**?*
*Could'**ja** help Steve?*	*No, could'**JU** help him?* **OR**	*No, could'**JU**?*

LET'S LEARN!

VOCABULARY

The following words and expressions were used in the previous dialogues. Let's take a closer look at what they mean.

blast (to have a) *exp.* to have a great time.

> **EXAMPLE:** We **had a blast** at the amusement park! We stayed there all day and night!
>
> **TRANSLATION:** We **had a great time** at the amusement park! We stayed there all day and night!
>
> **"REAL SPEAK":** We **had a blast** 'it the amusement park! We stayed there all day 'n night!
>
> *Variation:* **blast (to be a)** *exp.* to be a lot of fun, to be exciting.
>
> *Synonym 1:* **ball (to have a)** *exp.*
>
> *Synonym 2:* **way cool time (to have a)** *exp.* *(teen slang).*
>
> **NOW DO IT. COMPLETE THE PHRASE ALOUD:**
> *It was a blast going to...*

get a grip (to) *exp.* to get control of one's emotions.

> **EXAMPLE:** I've never seen you so upset! If you don't **get a grip**, you're going to get an ulcer!
>
> **TRANSLATION:** I've never seen you so upset! If you don't **get control of your emotions**, you're going to get an ulcer!
>
> **"REAL SPEAK":** I've never seen you so upset! If ya don't **ged a grip**, yer gonna ged 'n ulcer!
>
> *Note:* This expression refers to someone who is so upset that he/she needs "to get a grip" on his/her emotions.
>
> *Variation:* **get a grip on oneself (to)** *exp.*
>
> *Synonym 1:* **a hold of oneself (to get)** *exp.*
>
> *Synonym 2:* **pull oneself together (to)** *exp.*
>
> **NOW YOU DO IT. COMPLETE THE PHRASE ALOUD:**
> *Get a grip and stop...*

get a load of someone/something (to) *exp.* to take a good look at someone/something, to look at someone/something unusual or interesting.

> **EXAMPLE:** **Get a load of** the new dress Irene is wearing! I've never seen anything like it!
>
> **TRANSLATION:** **Look at** the new dress Irene is wearing! I've never seen anything like it!
>
> **"REAL SPEAK":** **Ged a load 'a** the new dress Irene's wearing! I've never seen anything like it!
>
> *Synonym:* **check out someone/something (to)** *exp.*
>
> **NOW YOU DO IT. COMPLETE THE PHRASE ALOUD:**
> *Get a load of that...*

get on someone's case (to) *exp.* to criticize or nag someone.

EXAMPLE:	Every time my aunt comes to visit, she **gets on my case** because I drive a motorcycle instead of a car.
TRANSLATION:	Every time my aunt comes to visit, she **nags** me because I drive a motorcycle instead of a car.
"REAL SPEAK":	Ev'ry time my aunt comes ta visit, she **gets on my case** 'cause I drive a modorcycle instead of a car.
Synonym:	**get on someone about something (to)** *exp.*

NOW YOU DO IT. COMPLETE THE PHRASE ALOUD:
My friends get on my case when I...

hunk *n.* a handsome and muscular man.

EXAMPLE:	David used to be very thin and weak. Now he's become a **hunk**!
TRANSLATION:	David used to be very thin and weak. Now he's become a **handsome and muscular man**!
"REAL SPEAK":	David usta be very thin 'n weak. Now 'e's become a **hunk**!
Synonym:	**stud** *n.*

NOW YOU DO IT. COMPLETE THE PHRASE ALOUD:
...is a real hunk!

No way! *interj.* • **1.** Absolutely not! • **2.** That's impossible!

EXAMPLE 1:	You want me to lend you money? **No way!** The last time you borrowed money from me, it took you a month to pay me back!
TRANSLATION:	You want me to lend you money? **Absolutely not!** The last time you borrowed money from me, it took you a month to pay me back!
"REAL SPEAK":	Ya want me da lend'ja money? **No way!** The las' time ya borrowed money fr'm me, it took ya a month ta pay me back!
EXAMPLE 2:	Todd just bought a new BMW?! **No way!** He doesn't have any money!
TRANSLATION:	Todd just bought a new BMW?! **That's impossible!** He doesn't have any money!
"REAL SPEAK":	Todd jus' bawd a new BMW?! **No way!** He doesn' have any money!
Note:	The difference between definitions **1.** and **2.** simply depends on the context.
Synonym:	**Get real!** *interj.*

NOW YOU DO IT. COMPLETE THE PHRASE ALOUD:
You just found ...?! No way!

put someone on (to) *exp.* to tease or kid someone.

EXAMPLE: I think Joe was **putting you on** when he said he has ten children. He just wanted to see your reaction.

TRANSLATION: I think Joe was **kidding you** when he said he has ten children. He just wanted to see your reaction.

"REAL SPEAK": I think Joe w'z **pudding you on** when 'e said 'e has ten children. He jus' wan'ed ta see yer reaction.

Synonym: **yank someone's chain (to)** *exp.*

NOW YOU DO IT. COMPLETE THE PHRASE ALOUD:
Susan was putting me on when she said...

rug *n.* (humorous/derogatory) hairpiece.

EXAMPLE: My father is starting to lose his hair. In another two years, he'll probably have to get a **rug**.

TRANSLATION: My father is starting to lose his hair. In another two years, he'll probably have to get a **hairpiece**.

"REAL SPEAK": My father's starding ta lose 'is hair. In another two years, 'e'll prob'ly hafta ged a **rug**.

NOW YOU DO IT. COMPLETE THE PHRASE ALOUD:
Bob wears a rug because...

unable to stand someone (to be) *exp.* to be unable to tolerate someone, to dislike.

EXAMPLE: I **can't stand** our new math teacher. She always gives us homework on the weekend.

TRANSLATION: I **can't tolerate** our new math teacher. She always gives us homework on the weekend.

"REAL SPEAK": I **can't stand** 'ar new math teacher. She always gives us homework on the weekend.

Synonym: **unable to stomach someone (to be)** *exp.*

NOW YOU DO IT. COMPLETE THE PHRASE ALOUD:
I can't stand Carl because...

What's up with... *exp.* What's the problem with... What's wrong with...

EXAMPLE: **What's up with** your brother? He looks really upset about something!

TRANSLATION: **What's the problem with** your brother? He looks really upset about something!

"REAL SPEAK": **What's up with** yer brother? He looks really upsed about something!

Synonym 1: **What's with...** *exp.*

Synonym 2: **What's the deal with...** *exp.*

NOW YOU DO IT. COMPLETE THE PHRASE ALOUD:
What's up with...?

LET'S PRACTICE!

A. CONTEXT EXERCISE *(Answers on p. 131)*

Read the short conversations. Decide whether the slang used makes sense or doesn't make sense. Circle your answer.

CD-A: TRACK 6

– Did you have fun at the party?
– Yes. I had a blast!

MAKES SENSE   DOESN'T MAKE SENSE

– I'm so upset!
– Get a grip. You need to relax.

MAKES SENSE   DOESN'T MAKE SENSE

–Bob is so thin!
–I know. He's such a hunk!

MAKES SENSE   DOESN'T MAKE SENSE

– You look beautiful today!
– Get off my case!

MAKES SENSE   DOESN'T MAKE SENSE

– My mother is a skydiver.
– You're putting me on!

MAKES SENSE   DOESN'T MAKE SENSE

– I thought Norman was bald.
– He is. He's wearing a rug!

MAKES SENSE   DOESN'T MAKE SENSE

– I can't stand Harriet!
– I like her, too!

MAKES SENSE   DOESN'T MAKE SENSE

– What's up with Steve?
– He's nervous about his grades.

MAKES SENSE   DOESN'T MAKE SENSE

– Get a load of Ann's dress?
– I did. It's so heavy!

MAKES SENSE   DOESN'T MAKE SENSE

B. CHOOSE THE RIGHT WORD (Answers on p. 131)

CD-A: TRACK 7

Underline the appropriate word that best completes the phrase.

1. Why are you so (**happy, relaxed, upset**)? I think you need to get a grip!

2. David is so (**thin, muscular, fat**). What a hunk!

3. You won a million dollars? Are you putting me (**on, off, in**)?

4. I had a (**bang, blast, boom**) at the party. It was so much fun!

5. What's (**up, down, over**) with the boss. He's been screaming at people all morning.

6. Did you get a load (**of, at, in**) that guy's haircut? It looks terrible.

7. I don't think his (**arm, hair, hand**) is real. I think it's a rug.

8. I can't stand Susan. She's always so (**nice, helpful, mean**) to me.

9. My mother got on my (**case, bag, wallet**) because I came home late last night.

10. That's your father? (**Yes, No, Maybe**) way! He looks so young!

C. COMPLETE THE PHRASE (Answers on p. 132)

CD-A: TRACK 8

Complete the phrase by choosing the appropriate words from the list below. Use each answer only once.

get a grip	**blast**	**rug**
putting me on	**no way**	**what's up**
on my case	**can't stand**	**hunk**

1. _____ with Tom? He's been in a bad mood all day.

2. I've never seen you so upset! _____!

3. Nancy gave birth to twins and she didn't even know she was pregnant?! I don't believe it. Are you _____?

4. My sister got _____ because I borrowed her sweater without asking.

5. I had a _____ at the amusement park!

6. I _____ our new math teacher. She gives us so much homework every weekend!

7. Carol asked you if she could borrow money again? _____! She borrows money from you every week!

8. I don't think his hair is real. I think it's a _____ .

9. Mike used to be so thin but he's turned into a real _____ .

D. IS IT "YES" OR IS IT "NO"? *(Answers on p. 132)*

Read Person A's questions aloud followed by the correct response from Person B. Use the suggested word(s) to create your answer.

PERSON A		PERSON B
1.	Do you think that Joe works out at the gym often?	Yes... [use: **hunk**]
2.	Do you like Stephanie?	No... [use: **can't stand**]
3.	You won a million dollars?! Are you serious?	No... [use: **putting you on**]
4.	Bob's hair looks so strange. Do you think it's real?	No... [use: **rug**]
5.	Did you notice how upset Jim is today?	Yes... [use: **get a grip**]
6.	Was the teacher mad you didn't do your homework?	Yes... [use: **got on my case**]
7.	Did you see that diamond necklace Cindy is wearing?	Yes... [use: **got a load of**]
8.	Did you know Kim is pregnant?	No... [use: **no way**]
9.	Did you have a good time at the carnival?	Yes... [use: **had a blast**]
10.	Did you notice what happened to Steve's eye?	Yes... [use: **what's up with**]

AT THE MARKET

"What a rip-off!"

LET'S WARM UP!

MATCH THE PICTURES *(Answers on p. 132)*

As a fun way to get started, see if you can guess the meaning of the new slang words and expressions on the opposite page by using the pictures below and following the context of the sentences.

1. Did you taste this blueberry pie? It's **to die for**!

2. Why did you pay so much for that TV? What **a rip-off**!

3. If you're ready, I can **ring up** your purchases.

4. This store has **rock bottom** prices.

5. The lines in this market are so long. They need more **checkers**.

6. The market is **slashing** its prices.

7. My mother always says I need to eat more **veggies**.

8. These pastries are **making my mouth water**.

9. My mother made a cake **from scratch**.

10. I need to **pick up** some milk at the market.

A. thievery

B. buy

C. absolutely fantastic

D. making me drool

E. add up

F. cashiers

G. extremely low

H. from the very beginning (using fresh ingredients)

I. vegetables

J. significantly reducing

LET'S TALK!

A. DIALOGUE USING SLANG & IDIOMS

The words introduced on the first two pages are used in the following dialogue and illustrated in the long picture above. Can you understand the conversation and find the illustration that corresponds to the slang? *Note*: The translation of the words in boldface is on the right-hand page.

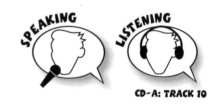

CD-A: TRACK 10

Bill and Liz are shopping for dinner.

Bill: Chicken is only twenty-nine cents a pound. Talk about **rock-bottom** prices!

Liz: I know. They've been **slashing** their prices all week.

Bill: I have an idea. Let's **pick up** some chicken and **veggies** and make a big salad tonight. We could also buy a cake for dessert.

Liz: Great idea! Look at this pastry section. It's **to die for**! Just look at all these cakes! The smell of these pastries is **making my mouth water**.

Bill: Wait! Did you see the price of these cakes? They cost more than the chicken. What a **rip-off**! Let's just make one **from scratch**. It'll be a lot cheaper.

Liz: I think you're right. Let's hurry and get the **checker** to **ring up** our purchases. I'm starving!

B. DIALOGUE TRANSLATED INTO STANDARD ENGLISH

LET'S SEE HOW MUCH YOU REMEMBER!
Just for fun, bounce around in random order to the words and
expressions in boldface below. See if you can remember their slang
equivalents without looking at the left-hand page!

Bill and Liz are shopping for dinner.

Bill: Chicken is only twenty-nine cents a pound. Talk about **extremely low** prices!

Liz: I know. They've been **significantly reducing** their prices all week.

Bill: I have an idea. Let's **buy** some chicken and **vegetables** and make a big salad tonight.
We could also buy a cake for dessert.

Liz: Great idea! Look at this pastry section. It's **fantastic**! Just look at all these cakes! The smell
of these pastries is **making me drool**.

Bill: Wait! Did you see the price of these cakes? They cost more than the chicken. What **thievery**!
Let's just make one **from the beginning using fresh ingredients**. It'll be a lot cheaper.

Liz: I think you're right. Let's hurry and get the **cashier** to **add up** our purchases. I'm starving!

C. DIALOGUE USING "REAL SPEAK"

The dialogue below demonstrates how the slang conversation on the previous page would *really* be spoken by native speakers!

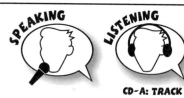

CD-A: TRACK 10

Bill 'n Liz'er shopping fer dinner.

Bill: Chicken's only twen'y-nine cents a pound. Talk about **rock-boddom** prices!

Liz: I know. They've been **slashing** their prices all week.

Bill: I have 'n idea. Let's **pick up** s'm chicken 'n **veggies** 'n make a big salad tanight. We could also buy a cake fer dessert.

Liz: Grade idea! Look 'it this pastry section. It's **ta die for**! Jus' look id all these cakes! The smell 'a these pastries is **making my mouth wader**.

Bill: Wait! Did'ja see the price of these cakes? They cost more th'n the chicken. Whad a **rip-off**! Let's jus' make one **fr'm scratch**. Id'll be a lot cheaper.

Liz: I think yer right. Let's hurry 'n get the **checker** da **ring up** 'ar purchases. I'm starving!

KEY TO "REAL SPEAK"

"T" = "D"

In the above dialogue using "real speak," "water" became "wader." Unlike British English, Americans commonly pronounce the letter "t" like a "d" in certain cases.

RULES

When a "t" is between two voiced vowels, the "t" is often pronounced like a soft "d" whether in a single word such as "city" (ci*d*y) or within a phrase such as "What a beautiful city!" (Wh*ad* *a* beau*d*iful ci*d*y).

HOW DOES IT WORK?

*Look **at** this pastry section.*
*Ok, b**ut** let's hurry.*
*Did you le**t** the dog out?*

} In these sentences, the "t" retains its sound. Why? Because in each case, there is a vowel on only one side of the "t."

(Great idea!)
*Gre**ad** **i**dea!*

(Did you invite Ellen to the party?)
*Did you invi**d**e Ellen to the party?*

} In these sentences, the "t" is pronounced as a "d" because in each case, there is a vowel on both sides of the "t."

BUT!

In many cases, when "t" is between an "n" and an "e," (or "y") the "t" is often silent, as seen in the real speak dialogue where "twenty" is pronounced "**twen'y**." Below are some other common examples:

prin**t**er = *prin'er*   complemen**t**ed = *complemen'ed*
cen**t**er = *cen'er*   coun**t**ed = *coun'ed*
en**t**ertainment = *en'ertainment*   presen**t**ed = *presen'ed*

KEY TO "REAL SPEAK"

...ED = 'D, 'T, OR 'ID?

When "ed" is added to a regular verb to form the past tense, the "ed" is pronounced **'d**, **'t**, or **'id** depending on what precedes it:

HOW DOES IT WORK?

...ed = 'd	**...ed = 't**	**...ed = 'id**
(after a voiced sound, meaning that you are making a sound which causes your vocal chords to vibrate rather than making a sound such as "sh" where your vocal chords do not move.)	*(after an unvoiced sound such as the sound of "sh," "k," "ss," etc. which do not involve your vocal chords.)*	*(after a "t" or "d")*
play**ed** tennis	slash**ed** prices	decid**ed** to go
travel**ed** to Paris	talk**ed** to him	add**ed** salt
order**ed** lunch	dress**ed** nicely	want**ed** money
deliver**ed** pizza	reduc**ed** cost	need**ed** rest
happen**ed** yesterday	increas**ed** sales	visit**ed** Tokyo

LET'S USE "REAL SPEAK!"

A. "T" PRONOUNCED LIKE "D" *(Answers on p. 132)*

CD-A: TRACK 11

STEP 1: Underline all instances where "t" is pronounced like "d."
STEP 2: Repeat the sentence aloud in real speak.

1. What a beautiful sweater! Did you get it when you went shopping last Saturday?

2. My parents ordered a bottle of champagne for their anniversary.

3. My laptop computer is battery-operated.

4. What a great car! Is it an automatic?

5. Let's go to the party later. Betty said there's going to be a lot of good food there.

6. What city do you live in?

7. Would you like a soft drink or a bottle of water?

8. Did you invite that pretty girl to your house for a little dinner?

9. I just bought a potted plant. It's a beautiful bonsai tree.

10. What a pity about your little sister's babysitter. I heard she got into a car accident!

LET'S LEARN!

SPEAKING LISTENING

CD-A: TRACK 12

VOCABULARY

The following words and expressions were used in the previous dialogues. Let's take a closer look at what they mean.

checker *n.* a cashier in a supermarket.

EXAMPLE:	Look at the long line in this market! They need more **checkers**.
TRANSLATION:	Look at the long line in this market! They need more **cashiers**.
"REAL SPEAK":	Look 'it the long line 'n this market! They need more **checkers**.
Note:	The *checker* works behind a *checkstand* where customers pay for their groceries.

NOW YOU DO IT. COMPLETE THE PHRASE ALOUD:
The checker at my grocery store always says...

from scratch (to make something) *exp.* • **1.** when used in reference to cooking, it means "to start or make something from the very beginning using fresh ingredients • **2.** (in general) to start something from the very beginning.

EXAMPLE 1:	Your daughter made this cake **from scratch**? When I was her age, I was using package mixes!
TRANSLATION:	Your daughter made this cake **starting from the very beginning using fresh ingredients**? When I was her age, I was using package mixes!
"REAL SPEAK":	Yer dauder made this cake **fr'm scratch**? When I w'z her age, I w'z using package mixes!
EXAMPLE 2:	I made a mistake on this drawing. Now I have to start over **from scratch**.
TRANSLATION:	I made a mistake on this drawing. Now I have to start over **from the very beginning**.
"REAL SPEAK":	I made a mistake on this drawing. Now I hafta stard over **fr'm scratch**.

NOW YOU DO IT. COMPLETE THE PHRASE ALOUD:
My mother makes ...from scratch.

make one's mouth water (to) *exp.* said of something that makes one drool.

EXAMPLE:	The smell of that fresh bread is **making my mouth water**!
TRANSLATION:	The smell of that fresh bread is **making me drool**!
"REAL SPEAK":	The smell 'a that fresh bread's **making my mouth wader**!

NOW YOU DO IT. COMPLETE THE PHRASE ALOUD:
The smell of ...makes my mouth water!

pick up (to) *v.* when in reference to going to the store, it means "to buy" or "to get."

EXAMPLE: I'm going to the market. Can I **pick up** something for you?

TRANSLATION: I'm going to the market. Can I **buy** something for you?

"REAL SPEAK": I'm going ta the market. C'n I **pick up** something for ya?

Synonym: **grab (to)** *v.* (lit.): to take.

NOW YOU DO IT. COMPLETE THE PHRASE ALOUD:
The last thing I picked up at the store was...

---

ring up (to) *v.* (said of a cashier) to add up, to tally.

EXAMPLE: I'm going to find a cashier **to ring up** my groceries.

TRANSLATION: I'm going to find a cashier **to add up** my groceries.

"REAL SPEAK": I'm gonna find a cashier **da ring up** my gros'ries.

Synonym: **check out (to)** *v.* • **1.** to add up a customer's purchases • **2.** to settle one's account at a grocery store or hotel • **3.** to look at, to observe.

EXAMPLE 1: My checkstand is open. I can **check you out** over here.

TRANSLATION: My checkstand is open. I can **add up your purchases** over here.

"REAL SPEAK": My checkstand's open. I can **check ya oud** over here.

EXAMPLE 2: We need to **check out** of the hotel early.

TRANSLATION: We need to **settle our account** at the hotel early.

"REAL SPEAK": We need ta **check oud** 'a the hotel early.

EXAMPLE 3: **Check out** that beautiful new car!

TRANSLATION: **Observe** that beautiful new car!

"REAL SPEAK": **Check out** that beaudiful new car!

NOW YOU DO IT. COMPLETE THE PHRASE ALOUD:
The cashier rang up my order of...

---

rip-off *n.* (said of something overpriced) thievery, theft.

EXAMPLE: You paid a thousand dollars for that television? What a **rip-off**! I saw an identical television yesterday for a hundred dollars!

TRANSLATION: You paid a thousand dollars for that television? What **thievery**! I saw an identical television yesterday for a hundred dollars!

"REAL SPEAK": You paid a thousan' dollers fer that TV? Whad a **rip-off**! I saw 'n idenical TV yesterday fer a hundred dollers!

Variation: **rip** *n.* a shortened version of: *rip-off.*

Also: **rip someone off (to)** *exp.*

NOW YOU DO IT. COMPLETE THE PHRASE ALOUD:
Having to pay ...dollars for ... is a rip-off!

rock-bottom

adj. (said of a price) extremely inexpensive.

EXAMPLE: I'm going to buy a new car today. The dealer is selling them at **rock-bottom** prices!

TRANSLATION: I'm going to buy a new car today. The dealer is selling them at **extremely low** prices!

"REAL SPEAK": I'm gonna buy a new car taday. The dealer's selling 'em at **rock-boddom** prices!

Synonym: **dirt-cheap** *adj.*

NOW YOU DO IT. COMPLETE THE PHRASE ALOUD:
My grocery store charges rock-bottom prices for...

slash prices (to) *exp.* to reduce prices significantly.

EXAMPLE: Do you want to go with me to the dress shop? They're **slashing their prices** today!

TRANSLATION: Do you want to go with me to the dress shop? They're **significantly reducing their prices** today!

"REAL SPEAK": Do ya wanna go with me da the dress shop? They're **slashing their prices** taday!

Synonym: **cut prices (to)** *exp.*

NOW YOU DO IT. COMPLETE THE PHRASE ALOUD:
The new market is slashing their prices on...

to die for *exp.* used to describe something that is wonderful (usually in reference to food or things).

EXAMPLE: I've never tasted such a wonderful pie in my life! It's **to die for**!

TRANSLATION: I've never tasted such a wonderful pie in my life! It's **absolutely fantastic**!

"REAL SPEAK": I've never tasted such a wonderful pie 'n my life! It's **ta die for**!

Variation: **to die from** *exp.*

NOW YOU DO IT. COMPLETE THE PHRASE ALOUD:
...is to die for!

veggies *n.* a popular shortened version of "vegetables."

EXAMPLE: My mother made a great dinner last night. She served chicken, rice, **veggies**, and a wonderful dessert.

TRANSLATION: My mother made a great dinner last night. She served chicken, rice, **vegetables**, and a wonderful dessert.

"REAL SPEAK": My mom made a great dinner las' night. She served chicken, rice, **veggies**, an' a wonderful dessert.

NOW YOU DO IT. COMPLETE THE PHRASE ALOUD:
My favorite veggies are...

LET'S PRACTICE!

A. TV COMMERCIAL *(Answers on p. 133)*

Read the commercial and answer the questions using a complete sentence.

WRITING

CD-A: TRACK 13

> Welcome to David's Market! In our produce department, we're **slashing our prices** on the largest selection of **veggies** in town. Make sure to visit our bakery where you can **pick up** our famous lemon cake. It's **to die for**! We also have everything you need to make a wonderful dessert **from scratch**! And best of all, you'll never have to wait in line because we have ten **checkers** waiting **to ring up** your order. So, come to David's market... your first choice in grocery shopping.

QUESTIONS:

1. **At David's Market, what do they have in the produce department?**

   Answer: _____

2. **Why won't you have to wait in line?**

   Answer: _____

3. **What did the announcer suggest that you pick up from the bakery?**

   Answer: _____

4. **Are they raising or lowering prices of vegetables at David's Market?**

   Answer: _____

5. **How is the lemon sponge cake in the bakery department?**

   Answer: _____

6. **If you prefer to make the cake yourself, does the market have what you need?**

   Answer: _____

B. YOU'RE THE AUTHOR *(Answers on p. 133)*
Complete the following dialogue using the word(s) from the
list below.

CD-A: TRACK 14

checker	mouth water	up	rock	to die for
scratch	pick up	rip-off	slashed	veggies

Joe: We need to _____ some _____ like lettuce, cucumber, and tomatoes for
our salad tonight. And you're going to love this store. They've _____ their
prices on everything this week.

Kim: You're right! I've never seen such _____-bottom prices. At my store, everything is so
expensive. Yesterday I paid five dollars for a loaf of bread! What a _____!

Joe: You're not kidding! Hey, I have an idea. Instead of buying dessert, let's make one from
_____...something with chocolate. I have a recipe that's _____!

Kim: You're making my _____! Let's buy the ingredients quickly so that we
can have the _____ ring _____ our order before I faint from hunger!

C. TRUE OR FALSE *(Answers on p. 133)*
Decide if the sentence is either true or false by checking the
appropriate box.

CD-A: TRACK 15

1. A **checker** works in a bank.
   ❏ True ❏ False

2. A hundred dollars for a candy bar is a **rip-off**.
   ❏ True ❏ False

3. If you paid a lot more this week for the same item last week, the market is **slashing** its prices.
   ❏ True ❏ False

4. The smell of hot bread cooking in the oven will **make your mouth water**.
   ❏ True ❏ False

5. A cake that doesn't taste good is **to die for**.
   ❏ True ❏ False

6. People who hate to bake prefer to make cakes **from scratch**.
   ❏ True ❏ False

7. People prefer to shop at stores that have **rock-bottom** prices.
   ❏ True ❏ False

8. A person who never eat carrots, corn, broccoli, or celery prefers to eat **veggies**.
   ❏ True ❏ False

9. A bank teller will **ring up** your order.
   ❏ True ❏ False

10. You can **pick up** a loaf of fresh bread at the bakery.
    ❏ True ❏ False

D. CROSSWORD PUZZLE *(Answers on p. 133)*

Fill in the crossword puzzle by choosing the correct word(s) from the list below.

CD-A: TRACK 16

rip	**slashed**	**ring**	**bottom**	**pick**
veggies	**die**	**checker**	**mouth**	**scratch**

ACROSS

1. You paid five hundred dollars for a pair of shoes? What a ____-off!
4. David's Market is having a huge sale today. They've ____ their prices on everything!
14. Let's find a ____ so we can pay for this food.
20. This store is known for having rock- ____ prices. You can always find some great deals here!
23. That dress is beautiful! It's to ____ for!

DOWN

1. If you've finished shopping, I'd be happy to ____ up your order for you.
3. Before we leave the market, I have to remember to ____ up some milk.
7. This cake is delicious! Did you make it from ____ ?
13. My horse loves ____, especially carrots.
18. The smell of this soup is making my ____ water!

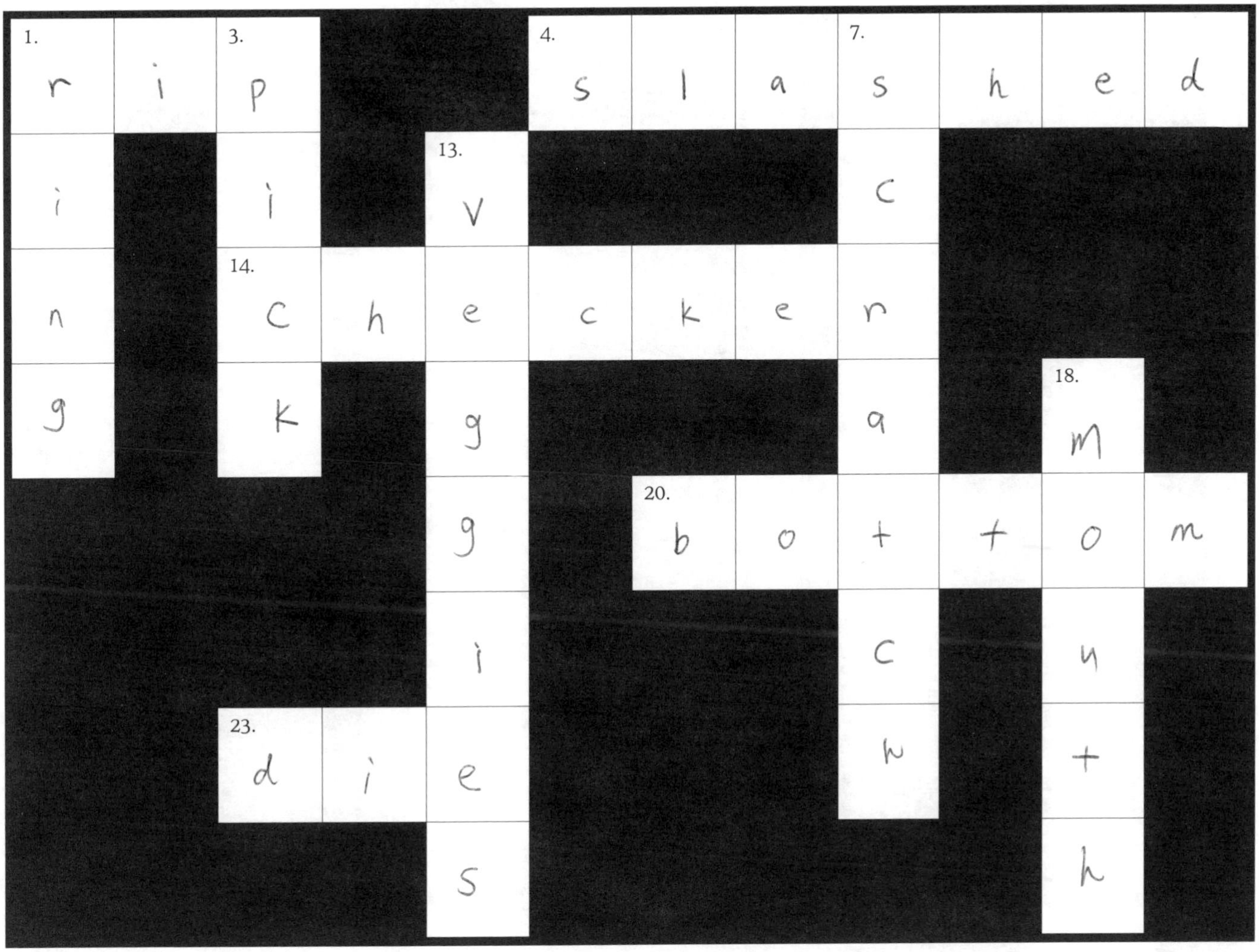

AT THE MOVIES

"Let's get the show on the road!"

LET'S WARM UP!

MATCH THE PICTURES *(Answers on p. 134)*

As a fun way to get started, see if you can guess the meaning of the new slang words and expressions on the opposite page by using the pictures below and following the context of the sentences. Each answer can only be used once!

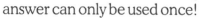

1. What a horrible actor! He **can't act his way out of a paper bag**.

   Definition: "is an excellent actor"

   ☐ True   ☐ False

2. What a great movie! It's going to be a real **blockbuster**!

   Definition: "failure"

   ☐ True   ☐ False

3. The critics loved the movie. They even gave it **two thumbs up**.

   Definition: "a bad review"

   ☐ True   ☐ False

4. That was the worst movie I've ever seen. What a **bomb**!

   Definition: "success"

   ☐ True   ☐ False

5. The movie was supposed to start ten minutes ago. Let's **get this show on the road**!

   Definition: "hurry and get started"

   ☐ True   ☐ False

6. Did you read the **write-up**? It's supposed to be a great movie.

   Definition: "review"

   ☐ True   ☐ False

7. There are no tickets left. It's a **sellout**.

   Definition: "performance for which all of the tickets have been sold"

   ☐ True   ☐ False

8. The movie is going to be very popular. It's being **plugged** all over the world!

   Definition: "promoted"

   ☐ True   ☐ False

9. That unpopular movie surprised everyone. It turned out to be a **sleeper**!

   Definition: "surprisingly successful movie"

   ☐ True   ☐ False

10. My role is too large! I have too many **lines** to memorize!

    Definition: "words in a script"

    ☐ True   ☐ False

LET'S TALK!

A. DIALOGUE USING SLANG & IDIOMS

The words introduced on the first two pages are used in the following dialogue and illustrated in the long picture above. Can you understand the conversation and find the illustration that corresponds to the slang? *Note*: The translation of the words in boldface is on the right-hand page.

CD-A: TRACK 17

George and David are at the movies.

George: It's a good thing we got tickets early. The movie is a **sellout**!

David: They must have been **plugging** this movie for weeks. Now it's a **blockbuster**!

George: The critics must be surprised that it turned out to be a **sleeper**.

David: I'll say. They said it was going to be a **bomb** and that the performers **couldn't act their way out of a paper bag.**

George: Well, yesterday I saw a **write-up** where the reviewer gave it **two thumbs up**. He said there were a lot of funny **lines**.

David: Reviewers never seem to agree on anything. When is this thing going to start? It should have started an hour ago. Let's **get the show on the road**!

B. DIALOGUE TRANSLATED INTO STANDARD ENGLISH

LET'S SEE HOW MUCH YOU REMEMBER!
Just for fun, bounce around in random order to the words and expressions in boldface below. See if you can remember their slang equivalents without looking at the left-hand page!

George and David are at the movies.

George: It's a good thing we got tickets early. The movie **doesn't have any tickets left**!

David: They must have been **promoting** this movie for weeks. Now it's a **huge success**!

George: The critics must be surprised that it turned out to be a **success after starting slowly**.

David: I'll say. They said it was going to be a **complete failure** and that the performers **couldn't act well at all**.

George: Well, yesterday I saw a **review** where the reviewer gave it **high praise**. He said there were a lot of funny **phrases in the script**.

David: Reviewers never seem to agree on anything. When is this thing going to start? It should have started an hour ago. Let's **start**!

C. DIALOGUE USING "REAL SPEAK"

The dialogue below demonstrates how the slang conversation on the previous page would *really* be spoken by native speakers!

CD-A: TRACK 17

George 'n David 'er at the movies.

George: It's a good thing we got tickets early. The movie's a **sellout**!

David: They must'a been **plugging** this movie fer weeks. Now it's a **blockbusder**!

George: The cridics must really be saprised thad it turned out ta be a **sleeper**.

David: Ah'll say. They said it w'z gonna be a **bomb** 'n th't the performers **couldn' act their way oud of a paper bag**.

George: Well, yesderday I saw a **wride-up** where the reviewer gave it **two thumbs up**. He said there were a lod 'a funny **lines**.

David: Reviewers never seem da agree on anything. When's this thing gonna start? It should'a starded 'n hour ago. Let's **get the show on the road**!

KEY TO "REAL SPEAK"

MUST HAVE = MUSTA

Musta is the most common reduction of "must have." However, don't be surprised if you also hear **must'ev** which is a popular variation.

RULES

Letters in an unstressed word (when the voice lowers in pitch) are often dropped when preceded by a stressed word (when the voice rises in pitch) as can be seen in the following example:

HOW DOES IT WORK?

They must have been plugging this movie for weeks!
> The up arrow indicates a stressed word and the down arrow indicates an unstressed word.

They must hav**e** been plugging this movie for weeks!
They must hav been plugging this movie for weeks!
> The "e" in "have" is silent.

They must **hav** been plugging this movie for weeks!
They must **a** been plugging this movie for weeks!
> In the combination "must have," "must" is always stressed and "have" is not. The "h" and "v" in "have" are dropped since they have a weaker (or less stressed) sound than the "a."

They must **a** been plugging this movie for weeks!
They must **uh** been plugging this movie for weeks!
> Unstressed short vowels (such as the remaining "a" in "have") are commonly pronounced **uh** but may be seen on occasion in print as **'a**, usually when quoting spoken language.

They must **'a** been plugging this movie for weeks!

KEY TO "REAL SPEAK"

WOULD'A · SHOULD'A · COULD'A

Other conditional verbs frequently follow the same pattern as **must'a** as seen with **would'a**, **should'a**, and **could'a**.

HOW DOES IT WORK?

would have = would'a	should have = should'a	could have = could'a
I **would'a** been a movie star.	I **should'a** been a movie star.	I **could'a** been a movie star.

LET'S USE "REAL SPEAK!"

WRITING

CD-A: TRACK 18

A. SHOULD'A, COULD'A, WOULD'A, MUST'A *(Answers on p. 134)*

Using the list below, fill in the blanks with the correct word(s). Note that one or more of the words in the list may be used more than once!

1. Jane didn't answer the phone. She _____ in the shower.

2. You _____ been there. The movie was great!

3. Look at all those packages. Lee _____ been shopping for hours!

4. Tom Cruise _____ an academy award for his last movie.

5. I _____ given that movie two thumbs up. It was horrible!

6. If they had called earlier, they _____ gone with us.

7. You _____ bought me such an expensive gift for my birthday.

8. Burt _____ lying or he _____ so nervous.

must'a been	wouldn'a been
must'a	wouldn'a
should'a gotten	could'a
should'a	shouldn'a

LET'S LEARN!

SPEAKING LISTENING

CD-A: TRACK 19

VOCABULARY

The following words and expressions were used in the previous dialogues. Let's take a closer look at what they mean.

...act one's ... way out of a paper bag (to be unable to) *exp.* to be a terrible actor.

BOO!

BOO!

EXAMPLE: I saw a terrible movie on television last night. The actors **couldn't act their way out of a paper bag**!

TRANSLATION: I saw a terrible movie on television last night. The actors **were horrible**!

"REAL SPEAK": I saw a terr'ble movie on TV las' night. The acters **couldn' act their way oud of a paper bag**!

NOW YOU DO IT. COMPLETE THE PHRASE ALOUD:
...can't act his/her way out of a paper bag.

blockbuster *n.* a very successful movie.

EXAMPLE: You have to go see the new movie that just opened. It's a real **blockbuster**!

TRANSLATION: You have to go see the new movie that just opened. It's a real **success**!

"REAL SPEAK": Ya hafta go see the new movie th't just opened. It's a real **blockbuster**!

Synonym 1: **hit** *n.*

Synonym 2: **smash** *n.*

Synonym 3: **smash-hit** *n.*

NOW YOU DO IT. COMPLETE THE PHRASE ALOUD:
The movie ...was a blockbuster!

bomb *n.* a complete failure (said of a movie, play, etc.).

BOOM!

EXAMPLE: Poor Gina. She produced a movie with her own money and it turned out to be a **bomb**.

TRANSLATION: Poor Gina. She produced a movie with her own money and it turned out to be a **complete failure**.

"REAL SPEAK": Poor Gina. She produced a movie with 'er own money 'n it turned out ta be a **bomb**.

Synonym: **dud** *n.*

Note: In the late nineties, teenagers created the expression *the bomb* meaning "fantastic":

...MPLE: That movie was **the bomb**!

TRANSLATION: That movie was **fantastic**!

"REAL SPEAK": That movie w'z **the bomb**!

NOW YOU DO IT. COMPLETE THE PHRASE ALOUD:
The last ...I saw was a bomb.

get the show on the road (to) *exp.* to begin something right away.

EXAMPLE: I can only stay at this meeting for thirty minutes, so **let's get the show on the road**.

TRANSLATION: I can only stay at this meeting for thirty minutes, so **let's begin right away**.

"REAL SPEAK": I c'n only stay at this meeding fer thirdy minutes, so **let's get the show on the road**.

NOW YOU DO IT. COMPLETE THE PHRASE ALOUD:
Let's get the show on the road! We're late for...

line *n.* a phrase or word that a performer memorizes from a script.

EXAMPLE: When I got hired to act in the movie, I thought it was going to be a very small part. But when I received the script, I discovered that I had pages and pages of **lines**!

TRANSLATION: When I got hired to act in the movie, I thought it was going to be a very small part. But when I received the script, I discovered that I had pages and pages of **phrases to memorize**!

"REAL SPEAK": When I got hired ta act in the movie, I thod it w'z gonna be a very small part. But when I received the script, I discovered th'd I had pages 'n pages of **lines**!

NOW YOU DO IT. COMPLETE THE PHRASE ALOUD:
...are the lines from (famous play or movie).

plug something (to) *v.* to advertise or promote something.

EXAMPLE: When the actor was interviewed on television, he **plugged** his new movie.

TRANSLATION: When the actor was interviewed on television, he **promoted** his new movie.

"REAL SPEAK": When the acter w'z in'erviewed on TV, he **plugged** 'is new movie.

Variation: **give something a plug (to)** *exp.*

NOW YOU DO IT. COMPLETE THE PHRASE ALOUD:
I saw a commercial on TV plugging...

sellout *n.* said of a performance for which all of the tickets have been sold.

EXAMPLE: I couldn't get tickets for the show at the Bijou tonight. It's a **sellout**!

TRANSLATION: I couldn't get tickets for the show at the Bijou tonight. **All of the tickets have been sold**!

"REAL SPEAK": I couldn't get tickets fer the show at the Bijou danight. It's a **sellout**!

NOW YOU DO IT. COMPLETE THE PHRASE ALOUD:
...was a sellout!

sleeper *n.* a success after starting slowly.

EXAMPLE: Megan's play was a bomb when it first opened, but it turned out to be a **sleeper**!

TRANSLATION: Megan's play was a bomb when it first opened, but it turned out to be a **success after starting slowly**!

"REAL SPEAK": Megan's play w'z a bomb when it first opened, bud it turned out ta be a **sleeper**!

NOW YOU DO IT. COMPLETE THE PHRASE ALOUD:

The movie ...was a sleeper.

two thumbs up (to give something) *exp.* to give something a favorable review.

EXAMPLE: Let's go see the movie around the corner. It should be really good. The critics **gave it two thumbs up**!

TRANSLATION: Let's go see the movie around the corner. It should be really good. The critics **gave it a favorable review**!

"REAL SPEAK": Let's go see the movie aroun' the corner. It should be really good. The cridics **gave it two thumbs up**!

Note: This expression comes from a popular television show featuring the two well-known critics, the late Gene Siskel and Roger Ebert, who gave individual critiques of movies. At the end of both reviews, the home audience was shown either a fist with a thumb pointing up (for a favorable review) or a fist with a thumb pointing down (for an unfavorable review) below each critic's name. Many times the critics were not in agreement. However, when both gave a favorable review, the audience was shown two thumbs up. This expression can also be used in reference to only *one* person's favorable review: *I give the movie two thumbs up!*

NOW YOU DO IT. COMPLETE THE PHRASE ALOUD:

I would give the movie ...two thumbs up!

write-up *n.* a written review of a play, show, etc.

EXAMPLE: Congratulations on your play! I read a great **write-up** about it in the Los Angeles Times!

TRANSLATION: Congratulations on your play! I read a great **review** about it in the Los Angeles Times!

"REAL SPEAK": C'ngradjalations on yer play! I read a great **wride-up** aboud id in the L.A. Times!

NOW YOU DO IT. COMPLETE THE PHRASE ALOUD:

I read a good/bad write up on...

LET'S PRACTICE!

A. I KNOW THE ANSWER, BUT WHAT'S THE QUESTION? _(Answers on p. 134)_

CD-A: TRACK 20

Read the answer and place a check next to the corresponding question.

1.

The answer is...

Yes. They loved it. They gave it two thumbs up.

Questions:
- ☐ Did Henry invite you to the opera?
- ☑ Did the critics enjoy the movie?
- ☐ Did your parents give you that book for your birthday?

2.

The answer is...

No. It was a sellout.

Questions:
- ☐ Were you able to find the movie theater?
- ☑ Were you able to get tickets for the play?
- ☐ Were you able to make a reservation at the restaurant?

3.

The answer is...

No. We have to get the show on the road.

Questions:
- ☑ Do we have time to eat something before we leave?
- ☐ Would you like mustard on your sandwich?
- ☐ Do you listen to classical music?

4.

The answer is...

Yes. They've been plugging it for weeks.

Questions:
- ☑ Do you want to go see the new musical _Felines_?
- ☐ Did you play drums in the concert last night?
- ☐ Is your piano brand new?

5.

The answer is...

No. I heard it was a bomb.

Questions:
- ☐ That movie was a failure, wasn't it?
- ☑ That movie made a fortune, didn't it?
- ☐ That movie was very long, wasn't it?

6.

The answer is...

It wasn't. But it turned out to be a sleeper.

Questions:
- ☑ Look at the long line! I thought you said this movie wasn't popular.
- ☐ Look at the long line! Do you think they still have tickets left?
- ☐ Look at the long line! Do you mind waiting to buy a ticket?

B. FIND YOUR PERFECT MATCH *(Answers on p. 134)*

Write the number of the slang term or idiom from Column A next to its matching picture in Column B as well as next to the matching definition in Column C.

READING

CD-A: TRACK 21

COLUMN A	COLUMN B	COLUMN C
1. to be unable to act one's way out of a paper bag	**3.**	**4.** to start something right away
2. a write-up	**4.** PUPPET SHOW	**2.** to give something a favorable review
3. to give something two thumbs up	**5.** GREAT MOVIE	**5.** to promote
4. to get the show on the road	**2.** THE END	**1.** to be a horrible actor
5. to plug	**1.** BOO! BOO!	**2.** a written review of a play, TV show, etc.

C. IMAGINE THAT... *(Answers on p. 135)*

Someone has presented you with a situation as seen below. Respond to each situation aloud by making a complete sentence using one of the groups of words below. Use each group only once.

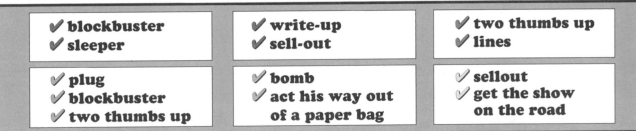

✔ blockbuster ✔ sleeper	✔ write-up ✔ sell-out	✔ two thumbs up ✔ lines

✔ plug
✔ blockbuster
✔ two thumbs up
	✔ bomb
	✔ act his way out
	   of a paper bag
		✔ sellout
		✔ get the show
		   on the road

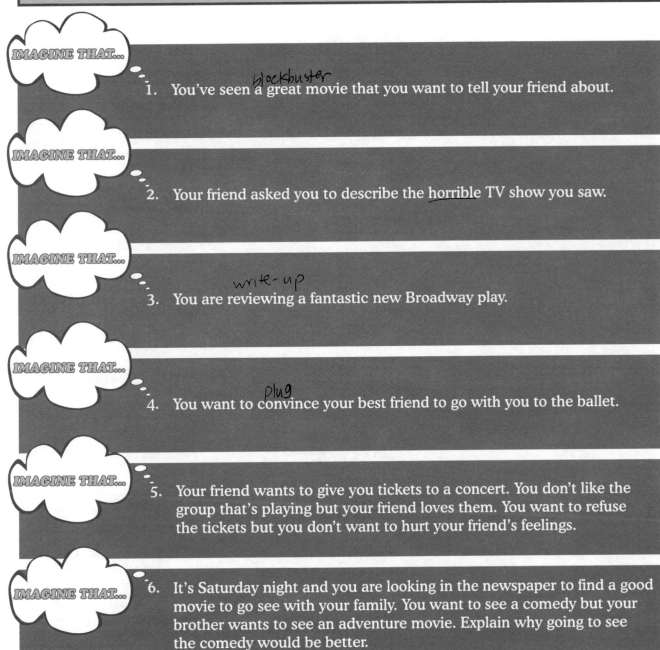

IMAGINE THAT...

1. You've seen a great movie that you want to tell your friend about. *blockbuster*

IMAGINE THAT...

2. Your friend asked you to describe the horrible TV show you saw.

IMAGINE THAT...

3. You are reviewing a fantastic new Broadway play. *write-up*

IMAGINE THAT...

4. You want to convince your best friend to go with you to the ballet. *plug*

IMAGINE THAT...

5. Your friend wants to give you tickets to a concert. You don't like the group that's playing but your friend loves them. You want to refuse the tickets but you don't want to hurt your friend's feelings.

IMAGINE THAT...

6. It's Saturday night and you are looking in the newspaper to find a good movie to go see with your family. You want to see a comedy but your brother wants to see an adventure movie. Explain why going to see the comedy would be better.

LESSON 4 ON VACATION

"Let's grab a cab and hit the town!"

LET'S WARM UP!

MATCH THE PICTURES (Answers on p. 135)

As a fun way to get started, see if you can guess the meaning of the new slang words and expressions on the opposite page by using the pictures below and following the context of the sentences.

1. Let's go to dinner tonight then **take in a movie**.
   - ❑ go to the movies
   - ❑ act in a movie

2. After working hard all week, it's nice to go to the beach and **hang out**.
   - ❑ play baseball
   - ❑ relax and do nothing

3. Instead of a hotel, let's stay in a **B and B**.
   - ❑ hotel with bed and breakfast
   - ❑ hotel with bath and beverage

4. Let's go to the pool and **take a dip**.
   - ❑ watch television
   - ❑ go swimming

5. You're so tan! Have you been **soaking up some sun** today?
   - ❑ staying inside
   - ❑ sunbathing

6. Let's **hit the town** and go shopping.
   - ❑ leave town
   - ❑ go into town

7. The hotel didn't have any rooms left. They were **booked solid**.
   - ❑ not yet cleaned
   - ❑ completely filled

8. I hope we can find a hotel **to put us up** for the night.
   - ❑ to lend us money
   - ❑ to accommodate us

9. In New York, you can either take the subway or **grab a cab** anywhere.
   - ❑ jump in front of a taxicab
   - ❑ take a taxicab

10. I'm tired because last night I **stayed up till all hours of the night**.
    - ❑ went to bed early
    - ❑ stayed awake until very late

11. I went **sightseeing** today. What a beautiful city!
    - ❑ visiting some interesting places
    - ❑ exercising

12. I usually get up early, but tomorrow I'm **sleeping in**.
    - ❑ getting up extra early
    - ❑ sleeping later than usual

LET'S TALK!

A. DIALOGUE USING SLANG & IDIOMS

The words introduced on the first two pages are used in the following dialogue and illustrated in the long picture above. Can you understand the conversation and find the illustration that corresponds to the slang? *Note:* The translation of the words in boldface is on the right-hand page.

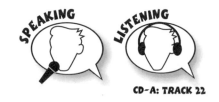

CD-A: TRACK 22

Chris and Marie are on vacation.

Chris: It's a good thing this **B&B** was able to **put us up** for the night. All the hotels in town were **booked solid**.

Marie: So, what should we do now? Hey, I have an idea. Tonight, let's **grab a cab** and **hit the town**. Maybe we can go **sightseeing** before dinner.

Chris: And since we're on vacation, we can **stay up till all hours of the night** and **sleep in** tomorrow.

Marie: Great! Then in the afternoon, we can **take a dip** and **hang out** by the pool. It'll be nice to **soak up some sun**.

Chris: And tomorrow night, we could **take in a movie**!

B. DIALOGUE TRANSLATED INTO STANDARD ENGLISH

LET'S SEE HOW MUCH YOU REMEMBER!
Just for fun, bounce around in random order to the words and expressions in boldface below. See if you can remember their slang equivalents without looking at the left-hand page!

Chris and Marie are on vacation.

Chris: It's a good thing this **hotel offering bed and breakfast** was able to **lodge us** for the night. All the hotels in town were **completely filled**.

Marie: So, what should we do now? Hey, I have an idea. Tonight, let's **take a taxicab** and **go into town**. Maybe we can go **visit the interesting places** before dinner!

Chris: And since we're on vacation, we can **stay awake until very late** and **sleep later than usual** tomorrow.

Marie: Great! Then in the afternoon, we can **go swimming** and **relax and do nothing** by the pool. It'll be nice to **sunbathe**.

Chris: And tomorrow night, we could **go to the movies**!

C. DIALOGUE USING "REAL SPEAK"

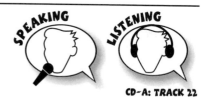

The dialogue below demonstrates how the slang conversation on the previous page would *really* be spoken by native speakers!

CD-A: TRACK 22

Chris 'n Marie 'er on vacation.

Chris: It's a good thing this **B 'n B** w'z able da **pud us up** fer the night. All the hotels 'n town were **booked solid**.

Marie: So, what shu'we do now? Hey, I have 'n idea. Tanight, let's **grab a cab** 'n **hit the town**. Maybe we c'n go **sightseeing** b'fore dinner.

Chris: An' since w'r on vacation, we c'n **stay up till all hours 'a the night** 'n **sleep in** tamorrow.

Marie: Great! Then in the afternoon, we c'n **take a dip** 'n **hang out** by the pool. Id'll be nice ta **soak up s'm sun**.

Chris: An' tamorrow night, we could **take in a movie**!

KEY TO "REAL SPEAK"

AND = 'N • IN = 'N

Since "and" and "in" are both reduced to **'n**, it can get a little confusing. That's why context is so important, as seen below.

RULES

Often in everyday conversation, when the word "and" connects two words, it is often pronounced **'n**. To add confusion, the preposition "in" is also pronounced **'n** when it follows a word. So, how do you know when the speaker means "and" or "in" since they are both pronounced the same? It all depends on the context.

HOW DOES IT WORK?

STANDARD ENGLISH	"REAL SPEAK"
and ▶	**'n**
Karen **and** Steve are coming to visit. At the zoo, I saw lions **and** tigers **and** bears.	Karen **'n** Steve are coming to visit. At the zoo, I saw lions **'n** tigers **'n** bears.
in ▶	**'n**
Tom is **in** Paris this week. Let's go **in** the house before it starts raining.	Tom is **'n** Paris this week. Let's go **'n** the house before it starts raining..

BUT!

If there is a pause before "and," it is commonly reduced to **an'** instead of **'n**. For example:

Today I'm visiting my mother in California...and tomorrow, I'm visiting my brother in New York!

Today I'm visiting my mother **'n** California...**an'** tomorrow, I'm visiting my brother **'n** New York!

LET'S USE "REAL SPEAK!"

A. PUT THE PAIRS BACK TOGETHER *(Answers on p. 135)*

Below are some common pairs of words that are often connected by "and." Find the missing piece on the right that completes the pair on the left. Make sure to pronounce "and" in real speak as 'n.

SPEAKING

CD-A: TRACK 23

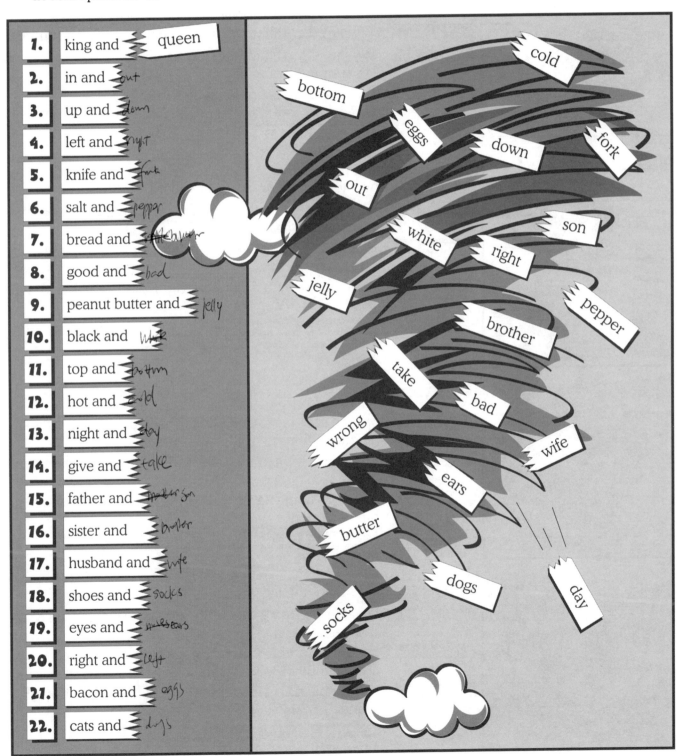

#		
1.	king and	queen
2.	in and	out
3.	up and	down
4.	left and	right
5.	knife and	fork
6.	salt and	pepper
7.	bread and	butter
8.	good and	bad
9.	peanut butter and	jelly
10.	black and	white
11.	top and	bottom
12.	hot and	cold
13.	night and	day
14.	give and	take
15.	father and	son
16.	sister and	brother
17.	husband and	wife
18.	shoes and	socks
19.	eyes and	ears
20.	right and	left
21.	bacon and	eggs
22.	cats and	dogs

LET'S LEARN!

CD-A: TRACK 24

VOCABULARY

The following words and expressions were used in the previous dialogues. Let's take a closer look at what they mean.

B and B  *n.* (an abbreviation for "bed and breakfast") generally a home converted into a hotel which offers guests a room for the night including breakfast.

> **EXAMPLE:** We stayed in a charming **B and B** in London last summer.
>
> **TRANSLATION:** We stayed in a charming **bed and breakfast** in London last summer.
>
> **"REAL SPEAK":** We stayed 'n a charming **B 'n B** 'n London las' summer.
>
> **NOW YOU DO IT. COMPLETE THE PHRASE ALOUD:**
> *If I owned a B and B, I would name it...*

booked solid (to be) *exp.* to be completely full, to have no more space available (said of a hotel, cruise ship, airplane, etc. that requires a reservation).

> **EXAMPLE:** I wanted to stay at the famous Ritz Hotel in Paris, but it was **booked solid**.
>
> **TRANSLATION:** I wanted to stay at the famous Ritz Hotel in Paris, but it was **completely full**.
>
> **"REAL SPEAK":** I wan'ed ta stay 'it the famous Ritz Hotel 'n Paris, bud it w'z **booked solid**.
>
> **NOW YOU DO IT. COMPLETE THE PHRASE ALOUD:**
> *I wanted to stay in a hotel in... but it was booked solid.*

grab  **a cab (to)** *exp.* to take a taxi.

> **EXAMPLE:** Instead of trying to find parking, let's just **grab a cab** and go out to dinner.
>
> **TRANSLATION:** Instead of trying to find parking, let's just **take a taxi** and go out to dinner.
>
> **"REAL SPEAK":** Instead 'a trying da fin' parking, let's jus' **grab a cab** 'n go out ta dinner.
>
> **NOW YOU DO IT. COMPLETE THE PHRASE ALOUD:**
> *It's best to grab a cab to go from .... to ...*

hang 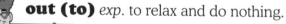 **out (to)** *exp.* to relax and do nothing.

> **EXAMPLE:** I'm going to **hang out** by the pool with Debbie today. Do you want to join us?
>
> **TRANSLATION:** I'm going to **relax and do nothing** by the pool with Debbie today. Do you want to join us?
>
> **"REAL SPEAK":** I'm gonna **hang out** by the pool with Debbie daday. Wanna join us?
>
> **NOW YOU DO IT. COMPLETE THE PHRASE ALOUD:**
> *I usually hang out at...*

hit the town (to) *exp.* to go into town where all the attractions are (usually for a night of fun, dining, dancing, movies, etc.).

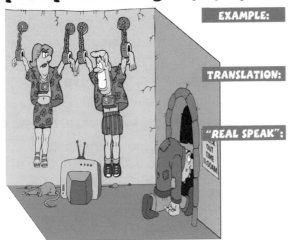

EXAMPLE: I'm bored tonight. I have an idea! Let's **hit the town** and go out to dinner and a movie!

TRANSLATION: I'm bored tonight. I have an idea! Let's **go into the main part of town** and go out to dinner and a movie!

"REAL SPEAK": I'm bored tanight. I have 'n idea! Let's **hit the town** 'n go out ta dinner 'n a movie!

NOW YOU DO IT. COMPLETE THE PHRASE ALOUD:
I like to hit the town and...

put up for the night (to) *exp.* to accommodate for the night.

EXAMPLE: We won't have to pay anything for a hotel when we go to Los Angeles. I have some friends there who can **put us up for the night**.

TRANSLATION: We won't have to pay anything for a hotel when we go to Los Angeles. I have some friends there who can **accommodate us for the night**.

"REAL SPEAK": We won't hafta pay anything fer a hotel when we go da L.A. I have s'm frien's there who c'n **pud us up fer the night**.

NOW YOU DO IT. COMPLETE THE PHRASE ALOUD:
When I go to ...'s house, he/she always puts me up for the night.

sightseeing (to go) *exp.* to go look at the attractions and interesting sights.

EXAMPLE: This is my first time in Rome. I can't wait **to go sightseeing**!

TRANSLATION: This is my first time in Rome. I can't wait **to go look at the attractions and interesting sights**!

"REAL SPEAK": This is my firs' time 'n Rome. I can't wait **ta go sightseeing**!

Variation: **sightsee (to)** *v.*

NOW YOU DO IT. COMPLETE THE PHRASE ALOUD:
I like going sightseeing in ...

sleep in (to) *exp.* to sleep later than usual.

EXAMPLE: Everyday, I wake up at six o'clock in the morning. But next week when I'm on vacation, I'm going to **sleep in**!

TRANSLATION: Everyday, I wake up at six o'clock in the morning. But next week when I'm on vacation, I'm going to **sleep later than usual**!

"REAL SPEAK": Ev'ryday, I wake up 'it six a'clock 'n the morning. B't next week when I'm on vacation, I'm gonna **sleep in**!

NOW YOU DO IT. COMPLETE THE PHRASE ALOUD:
I like to sleep in until...

soak up some sun (to) *exp.* to sunbathe.

EXAMPLE: I'm going to Hawaii tomorrow! I'm not going to do anything but **soak up some sun** and relax!

TRANSLATION: I'm going to Hawaii tomorrow! I'm not going to do anything but **sunbathe** and relax!

"REAL SPEAK": I'm going da Hawaii damorrow! I'm not gonna do anything b't **soak up s'm sun** 'n relax!

Synonym 1: **soak up some rays (to)** *exp.*

Synonym 2: **catch some rays (to)** *exp.*

NOW YOU DO IT. COMPLETE THE PHRASE ALOUD:
...is a great place to soak up some sun!

stay up till all hours of the night (to) *exp.* to stay up all night long (having a good time, studying, watching television, etc.).

EXAMPLE: The party went on for hours! We **stayed up till all hours of the night** dancing!

TRANSLATION: The party went on for hours! We **stayed up all night** dancing!

"REAL SPEAK": The pardy wen' on fer hours! We **stayed up till all hours 'a the night** dancing!

NOW YOU DO IT. COMPLETE THE PHRASE ALOUD:
I stayed up till all hours of the night doing...

take a dip (to) *exp.* to go swimming.

EXAMPLE: It's such a beautiful warm day today. I think I'll **take a dip**.

TRANSLATION: It's such a beautiful warm day today. I think I'll **go swimming**.

"REAL SPEAK": It's such a beaudif'l warm day daday. I think ah'll **take a dip**.

Synonym: **go for a swim (to)** *exp.*

NOW YOU DO IT. COMPLETE THE PHRASE ALOUD:
Last summer I took a dip when I went to...

take in a movie (to) *exp.* to go to the movies.

EXAMPLE: It's been raining all day long. Well, since we can't do anything outside, do you want to **take in a movie**?

TRANSLATION: It's been raining all day long. Well, since we can't do anything outside, do you want to **go to the movies**?

"REAL SPEAK": It's been raining all day long. Well, since we can't do anything outside, wanna **take in a movie**?

NOW YOU DO IT. COMPLETE THE PHRASE ALOUD:
The last time I took in a movie, I saw...

LET'S PRACTICE!

A. FIND THE MISSING WORDS (Answers on p. 136)
Complete the dialogue by filling in the blanks with the correct word(s) using the list below.

CD-A: TRACK 25

put us up	town	hang out
B&B	sightseeing	soak up
solid	sleep	take in
grab	dip	hours of the night

Tom: This __B&B__ has so much more charm than the hotel we stayed at last night.

Becky: It's a good thing they were able to __put us up__ for the night. It was the only vacancy in the entire city! All the other places were booked __solid__ .

Tom: We really got lucky. It's so quiet here. It was hard to __sleep__ in at the other hotel because of all the noise. So, what do you want to do tonight?

Becky: Let's go hit the __town__ !

Tom: Good idea. We could go __take in__ a movie.

Becky: Actually, I thought it would be fun to go __sightseeing__ and explore a little. We could __grab__ a cab and be there in a few minutes.

Tom: After we visit the sites, we could get something to eat at that great restaurant around the corner and then go dancing till all __hours of the night__ .

Becky: That's perfect! Then tomorrow we could relax all day. It would be so nice to wake up late then __hang out__ by the pool and __soak up__ some sun. We could even take a __dip__ if it's gets too hot!

B. **MATCH THE SENTENCES** (Answers on p. 136)

Match the numbered sentences below with the lettered sentences on the opposite page. Write your answers in the boxes at the bottom of the pages.

READING

CD-A: TRACK 26

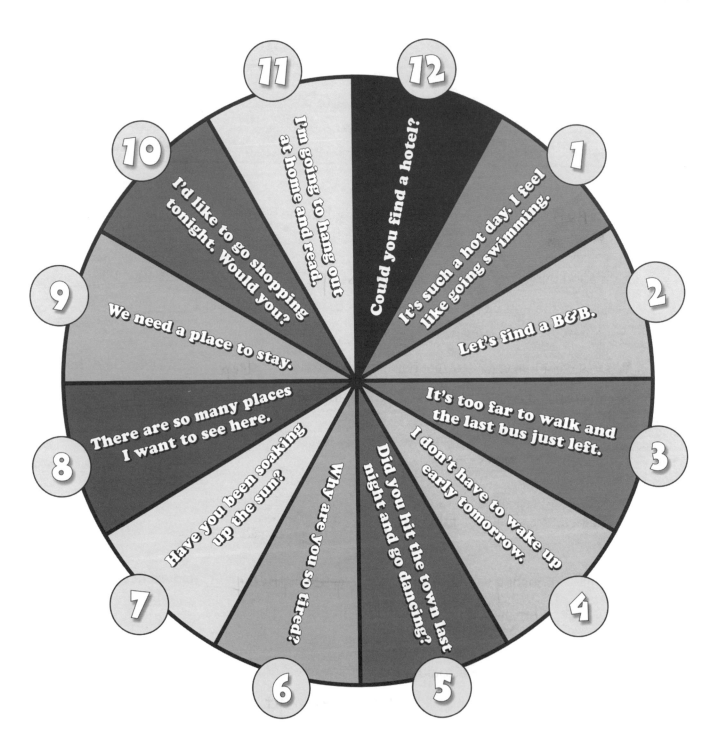

Could you find a hotel?

It's such a hot day. I feel like going swimming.

Let's find a B&B.

It's too far to walk and the last bus just left.

I don't have to wake up early tomorrow.

Did you hit the town last night and go dancing?

Why are you so tired?

Have you been soaking up the sun?

There are so many places I want to see here.

We need a place to stay.

I'd like to go shopping tonight. Would you?

I'm going to hang out at home and read.

NUMBERS	1	2	3	4	5	6
LETTERS	F	J	D	I	A	B

B. MATCH THE SENTENCES - *(continued)*

CD-A: TRACK 26

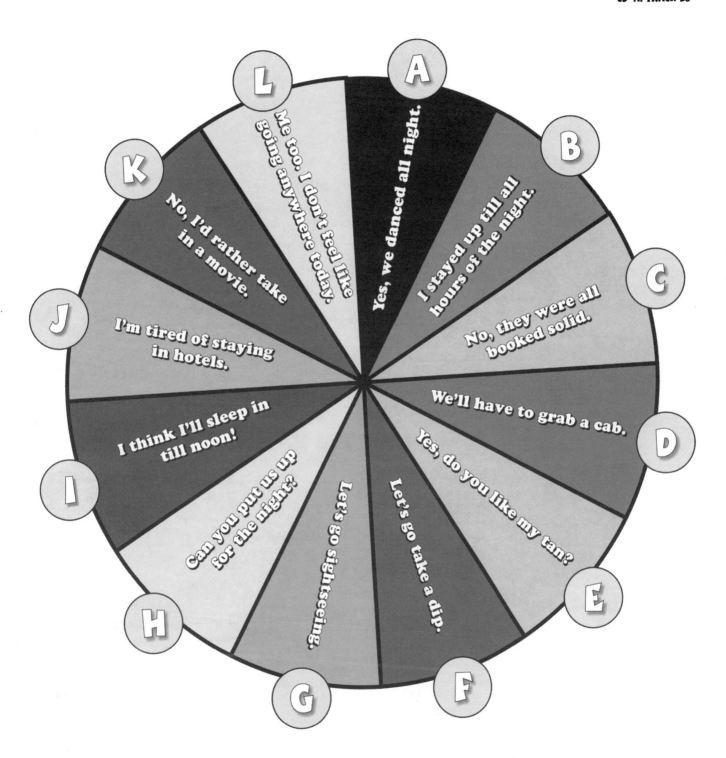

A — Yes, we danced all night.

B — I stayed up till all hours of the night.

C — No, they were all booked solid.

D — We'll have to grab a cab.

E — Yes, do you like my tan?

F — Let's go take a dip.

G — Let's go sightseeing.

H — Can you put us up for the night?

I — I think I'll sleep in till noon!

J — I'm tired of staying in hotels.

K — No, I'd rather take in a movie.

L — Me too. I don't feel like going anywhere today.

NUMBERS	7	8	9	10	11	12
LETTERS	E	G	H	K	L	C

LESSON 5 — AT THE AIRPORT

"I'm taking the red-eye"

LET'S WARM UP!

MATCH THE PICTURES *(Answers on p. 136)*

As a fun way to get started, see if you can guess the meaning of the new slang words and expressions on the opposite page by using the pictures below and following the context of the sentences.

READING

I 1. I hate taking the **red-eye**. I always arrive so tired.

K 2. I don't take a lot of clothes with me when I go on business trips. I prefer to **travel light**.

C 3. Since I didn't have a reservation, I was put on **standby**.

J 4. I **got bumped** because I was late to the airport.

A 5. I'm sorry I'm late. We had a three-hour **layover** in Texas.

F 6. As a **frequent flyer**, I was given a free ticket!

D 7. I got sick during the flight and needed a **barf bag**.

H 8. After not sleeping all night, I'm **wiped out**.

L 9. When I arrived in Paris, I was **wired** because I was so excited!

B 10. When you fly from L.A. to New York, do you get **jet lag**?

E 11. Lois lives **way out in the boonies**. I got lost five times on the way to her house!

G 12. It's easier to travel with only a **carry-on**.

A. stop

B. tired from crossing time zones

C. a passenger waiting list

D. bag used for airsickness

E. in a distant and remote location

F. person who travels often

G. small suitcase that can be carried on the plane

H. exhausted

I. overnight flight

J. lost my seat in the airplane

K. travel with few items

L. full of energy

LET'S TALK!

A. DIALOGUE USING SLANG & IDIOMS

The words introduced on the first two pages are used in the following dialogue and illustrated in the long picture above. Can you understand the conversation and find the illustration that corresponds to the slang? *Note*: The translation of the words in boldface is on the right-hand page.

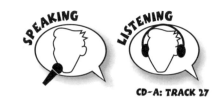

SPEAKING LISTENING

CD-A: TRACK 27

Karen is at the airport waiting for Steve to arrive.

Steve: I'm sorry we're so late. We had an unexpected two-hour **layover** some place **way out in the boonies**. You know, I almost missed the flight entirely because of all the traffic! So I arrived late and **got bumped**. Luckily, they agreed to put me on **standby**. All I had was a **carry-on**, so it was easy.

Karen: It's a good thing you **travel light**. Well, with the **jet lag**, I imagine you're pretty **wiped out**.

Steve: Actually, I'm pretty **wired** after all that traveling. At least I got a free ticket for being a **frequent flyer**!

Karen: So, how was it traveling on the **red-eye**?

Steve: It got a little bumpy for a while. Luckily, I never had to use the **barf bag**!

B. DIALOGUE TRANSLATED INTO STANDARD ENGLISH

LET'S SEE HOW MUCH YOU REMEMBER!
Just for fun, bounce around in random order to the words and expressions in boldface below. See if you can remember their slang equivalents without looking at the left-hand page!

Karen is at the airport waiting for Steve to arrive.

Steve: I'm sorry we're so late. We had an unexpected two-hour **stop** some place **far away and remote**. You know, I almost missed the flight entirely because of all the traffic! So I arrived late and **my seat was given away**. Luckily, they agreed to put me on **a waiting list**. All I had was a **bag small enough to take on the airplane**, so it was easy.

Karen: It's a good thing you **travel with little luggage**. Well, with the **fatigue due to the time difference**, I imagine you're pretty **exhausted**.

Steve: Actually, I'm pretty **tense with excitement** after all that traveling. At least I got a free ticket for being a **regular airline traveler**!

Karen: So, how was it traveling on the **overnight flight**?

Steve: It got a little bumpy for a while. Luckily, I never had to use the **airsickness bag**!

C. DIALOGUE USING "REAL SPEAK"

The dialogue below demonstrates how the slang conversation on the previous page would *really* be spoken by native speakers!

CD–A: TRACK 27

Karen's at the airport waiding fer Steve ta arrive.

Steve: I'm sorry w'r so late. We had 'n unexpected two-hour **layover** some place **way out 'n the boonies**. Ya know, I almost missed the flide entirely 'cuz of all the traffic! So I arrived late 'n **got bumped**. Luckily, they agreed da put me on **stan'by**. All I had w'z a **carry-on**, so it w'z easy.

Karen: It's a good thing ya **travel light**. Well, with the **jet lag**, I imagine yer preddy **wiped out**.

Steve: Akshelly, I'm preddy **wired** after all that trav'ling. At least I godda free ticket fer being a **frequent flyer**!

Karen: So, how w'z it trav'ling on the **red-eye**?

Steve: It god a liddle bumpy fer a while. Luckily, I never had ta use the **barf bag**!

KEY TO "REAL SPEAK"

TO = "TA" OR "DA"

As seen in the "real speak" dialogue above, the reduction of "to" to **ta** and **da** is used by everyone!

RULES

Often in everday conversation, "to" is pronounced "**ta**" when following an unvoiced consonant (*meaning a sound such as "sh," "k," "b," "g," "t," "ss," etc., which does not involve your vocal chords*).

However, when following either a voiced consonant (*meaning a sound which causes your vocal chords to vibrate*), a vowel, or the letter "d," "to" is often pronounced "**da**."

NOTE: The "d" in **da** is not pronounced as strongly as the "d" in "dog," for example. It is much softer as demonstrated throughout the audio program.

HOW DOES IT WORK?

TO = TA ("to" follows an unvoiced sound)	TO = DA ("to" follows a voiced consonant, a vowel, or the letter "d")
How much will it cos**t ta** ride the bu**s ta** work?	I tr**y da** do a good job at work.
I'd li**ke ta** take a tri**p ta** Tokyo this summer.	Do you know the wa**y da** Hollywood from here?
He wen**t ta** Pari**s ta** study this year.	Don't ask m**e da** do that again!
We walke**d ta** the par**k ta** feed the pigeons.	Do you know ho**w da** fix the toaster?
We stoppe**d ta** have something **ta** eat.	Brush your teeth before you g**o da** the dentist.
Nancy want**s ta** invite Caro**l ta** the party.	You ran all the wa**y da** John's house? That's far!
Betsy skippe**d ta** school.	I nee**d da** g**o da** my aunt's house.

LET'S USE "REAL SPEAK!"

A. "ACROSS" WORD PUZZLE *(Answers on p. 137)*

The following sentences are written in "real speak." Rewrite the entire sentence in standard English using one letter per box.

CD-A: TRACK 28

Will ya go da the market ta get me something ta eat?

1. | W | i | l | l | | Y | o | u | | g | o | | t | o | | t | h | e | | m | a | r | k | e | t |
| t | o | | g | e | t | | m | e | | s | o | m | e | t | h | i | n | g | | t | o | | e | a | t | ? |

I have ta try da find a present ta give ta my wife.

2. | I | | h | a | v | e | | t | o | | t | r | y | | t | o | | f | i | n | d | | a |
| p | r | e | s | e | n | t | | t | o | | g | i | v | e | | t | o | | m | y | | w | i | f | e | . |

Ya need da know how da drive in order da buy a car.

3.

If I need ya da help me move tamorrow, I'll ask.

4.

It's really too cold da go da the beach this morning.

5.

B. "TA BE" OR NOT "TA BE..." *(Answers on p. 137)*

Say the following sentences in real speak deciding when to use "ta" and when to use "da."

CD-A: TRACK 29

1. I went **to**(ta) the market **to**(ta) pick up some bread.

2. Can you tell me how **to**(da) get **to**(ta) the post office from here?

3. Steve wanted **to**(da) go **to**(da) the park but I wanted **to**(da) go shopping instead.

4. I'd love **to**(da) join you but I have work **to**(ta) do.

5. On the way **to**(da) the airport, I had **to**(da) stop **to**(ta) get gas.

6. We need **to**(da) close the windows before it starts **to**(ta) rain.

7. I don't like **to**(da) go **to**(da) the dentist.

8. Jennifer's two friends were too tired **to**(da) go **to**(da) the movies.

LET'S LEARN!

VOCABULARY

The following words and expressions were used in the previous dialogues. Let's take a closer look at what they mean.

barf bag n. a bag used for air sickness (usually in the back pocket of the seat in front of the passenger).

> **EXAMPLE:** I sat next to a man who was airsick during the entire flight. He never stopped using the **barf bag**.
>
> **TRANSLATION:** I sat next to a man who was airsick during the entire flight. He never stopped using the **airsickness bag**.
>
> **"REAL SPEAK":** I sat next to a man who w'z airsick during the entire flight. He never stopped using the **barf bag**.

NOW YOU DO IT. COMPLETE THE PHRASE ALOUD:
An unusual use for a barf bag is...

boonies (way out in the) n. in a place that is far away and remote.

> **EXAMPLE:** My grandmother lives **way out in the boonies**. It takes us hours to get to her house.
>
> **TRANSLATION:** My grandmother lives **in a far away and remote place**. It takes us hours to get to her house.
>
> **"REAL SPEAK":** My gramma lives **way oud 'n the boonies**. It takes us hours da get to 'er house.
>
> *Synonym:* **boondocks (way out in the)** n.

NOW YOU DO IT. COMPLETE THE PHRASE ALOUD:
My friend ...lives way out in the boonies.

bumped (to get) v. to lose one's seat in an airplane, train, etc.

> **EXAMPLE:** I **got bumped** for being five minutes late! Now I have to take a later flight.
>
> **TRANSLATION:** I **lost my seat** for being five minutes late! Now I have to take a later flight.
>
> **"REAL SPEAK":** I **got bumped** fer being five minutes late! Now I hafta take a lader flight.
>
> *Also:* **bumped up (to get)** v. to get upgraded to a higher class of travel.

NOW YOU DO IT. COMPLETE THE PHRASE ALOUD:
When I was traveling to ...I got bumped.

carry-on n. a small bag which one can easily "carry on" and place in the airplane.

> **EXAMPLE:** When you go to Paris for the week, just take a **carry-on**. That way you can avoid the long line at baggage claim.
>
> **TRANSLATION:** When you go to Paris for the week, just take a **small bag which you can easily carry with you on the airplane**. That way you can avoid the long line at baggage claim.
>
> **"REAL SPEAK":** When ya go da Paris fer the week, jus' take a **carry-on**. That way you c'n avoid the long line 'it baggage claim.

NOW YOU DO IT. COMPLETE THE PHRASE ALOUD:
In my carry-on, I always pack my...

frequent flyer *n.* a person who travels often by air and is part of a special program offering free flights for those who travel frequently.

EXAMPLE: As a **frequent flyer**, I can get a free ticket to anywhere in the world after I've traveled 100,000 miles!

TRANSLATION: As a **member of the airline's special program offering free flights for those who travel often**, I can get a free ticket to anywhere in the world after I've traveled 100,000 miles!

"REAL SPEAK": As a **frequent flyer**, I c'n ged a free ticket ta anywhere 'n the world after I've traveled 100,000 miles!

NOW YOU DO IT. COMPLETE THE PHRASE ALOUD:
As a frequent flyer, I got a free trip to...

jet lag *n.* fatigue due to the time change between one's point of departure and one's destination.

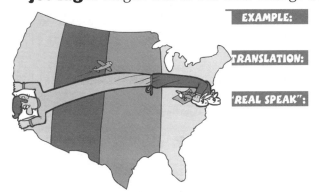

EXAMPLE: I never get **jet lag** when I travel to Europe. But when I travel back home, I'm exhausted!

TRANSLATION: I never get **tired from the time change** when I travel to Europe. But when I travel back home, I'm exhausted!

"REAL SPEAK": I never get **jet lag** when I travel da Europe. B't when I travel back home, I'm exhausted!

NOW YOU DO IT. COMPLETE THE PHRASE ALOUD:
The worst jet lag I had was when I traveled to...

layover *n.* a stop in one or more cities when traveling by air.

EXAMPLE: On our way to Paris, we had a three-hour **layover** in Amsterdam.

TRANSLATION: On our way to Paris, we had a three-hour **stop** in Amsterdam.

"REAL SPEAK": On 'ar way da Paris, we had a three-hour **layover** 'n Amsterdam.

NOW YOU DO IT. COMPLETE THE PHRASE ALOUD:
The longest layover I ever had was...

red-eye *n.* a flight which occurs overnight and whose passengers arrive at their destination with "red eyes" from staying awake.

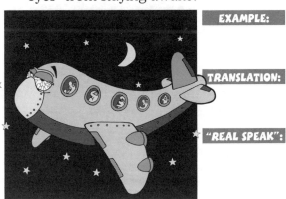

EXAMPLE: I'm taking the **red-eye** to New York instead of taking a flight during the daytime because I can save a lot of money.

TRANSLATION: I'm taking the **overnight flight** to New York instead of taking a flight during the daytime because I can save a lot of money.

"REAL SPEAK": I'm taking the **red-eye** ta New York instead of taking a flight during the daytime 'cuz I c'n save a lod 'a money.

NOW YOU DO IT. COMPLETE THE PHRASE ALOUD:
The last time I took a red-eye was...

standby (to be on)

n. to be on a passenger waiting list for an available seat.

EXAMPLE: Since I didn't have a reservation, the airline put me on **standby**.

TRANSLATION: Since I didn't have a reservation, the airline put me on **a passenger waiting list for an available seat**.

"REAL SPEAK": Since I didn't have a reservation, the airline put me on **stan'by**.

NOW YOU DO IT. COMPLETE THE PHRASE ALOUD:
I would fly standby if...

travel light (to)

exp. to travel with few pieces of luggage (usually only a small piece of luggage).

EXAMPLE: I always **travel light**, even when I go overseas. Then I can buy lots of souvenirs!

TRANSLATION: I always **travel with a small light piece of luggage**, even when I go overseas. Then I can buy lots of souvenirs!

"REAL SPEAK": I always **travel light**, even when I go overseas. Then I c'n buy lots 'a souvenirs!

NOW YOU DO IT. COMPLETE THE PHRASE ALOUD:
When I travel light, I never pack my...

wiped out (to be) *adj.* to be exhausted.

EXAMPLE: After traveling for two days, I'm **wiped out**. All I want to do is to go to bed!

TRANSLATION: After traveling for two days, I'm **exhausted**. All I want to do is to go to bed!

"REAL SPEAK": After trav'ling fer two days, I'm **wiped out**. All I wanna do is ta go da bed!

NOW YOU DO IT. COMPLETE THE PHRASE ALOUD:
I'm wiped out because...

wired (to be) *exp.* to be tense with excitement.

EXAMPLE: After all of this excitement today, I don't know how I'm going to sleep tonight. I'm so **wired**!

TRANSLATION: After all of this excitement today, I don't know how I'm going to sleep tonight. I'm so **tense with excitement**!

"REAL SPEAK": After all 'a this excitement taday, I dunno how I'm gonna sleep tanight. I'm so **wired**!

Synonym: **buzzed (to be)** *adj.* • **1.** to be extremely energetic • **2.** to be slightly intoxicated.

NOW YOU DO IT. COMPLETE THE PHRASE ALOUD:
I'm wired because...

LET'S PRACTICE!

A. COMPLETE THE FAIRY TALE *(Answers on p. 137)*

Fill in the blanks by choosing the correct word from the list below. Note that two extra words are in the list from the previous lesson!

WRITING

CD-A: TRACK 31

Once upon a time, there was a young girl named Cinderella who lived way out in the _boonies_ and wanted something fun to do. So one day, she decided to use her frequent _flyer_ miles and get a free ticket to somewhere exciting. She made an appointment to sell her script to a big producer in Hollywood. She always thought that her life story would make a good movie or even a musical!

Later that day, taking only a _carry_-on, she left for the airport. She always believed in _travel_ light. Unfortunately, when she arrived at the airport, she got _bumped_ because she was late. So, she was put on _standby_ for the next available flight. Finally, several hours later and completely wiped _out_, she was put on the _red_-eye for Hollywood, California!

The flight was so bumpy, that she started to feel airsick and feared that she might have to use the _barf_ bag. Fortunately, just then the plane made a landing in Denver. After a two-hour _layover_, she was once again on her way to Hollywood, the land of fame and fortune.

By the time she arrived, she was so _wired_ that she couldn't sleep and stayed up till all _hours_ of the night. Unfortunately, the combination of no sleep and jet _lag_ caused her to _sleep_ in late and miss her appointment with the producer!

She was so disappointed that she decided to take the next flight back home. However, as fate would have it, she found herself sitting in the airplane next to Howard, a very handsome young man, formerly known as Prince.

Cinderella and Howard, formerly known as Prince, fell in love and moved to Chicago where they lived happily ever after in a double-wide mobile home.

wired	**traveling**	**out**
boonies	**bumped**	**red**
flyer	**hours**	**sleep**
carry	**standby**	**barf**
layover	**lag**	

B. CONTEXT EXERCISE *(Answers on p. 138)*
Look at the phrase in the left column then find the best match
in the right column. Write the appropriate letter in the box.

CD-A: TRACK 32

K 1. Why don't you visit Nancy more
often?

L 2. I thought you left for Los Angeles
today. What happened?

B 3. Why are you so tired?

C 4. I hope you'll come visit me when you
come through London.

G 5. It was hard traveling with so many
suitcases.

A 6. There was so much turbulence on the
plane that I got airsick.

D 7. You're only taking that little suitcase
on your trip?

I 8. It's midnight but I'm not tired. It's
three hours earlier where I arrived
from. But I know I'll be tired when I
wake up tomorrow morning.

F 9. I haven't slept in two days because
I've been traveling. I'm looking
forward to going to bed.

J 10. It didn't cost me anything to fly here!

L 11. I wasn't able to buy a ticket for this
flight.

H 12. I shouldn't have had so much coffee
on the plane.

A. It was the first time I ever
needed a **barf bag**.

B. I'm so **wiped out**.

C. I'm afraid I'll only be there for a
ten-minute **layover**.

D. Yes. I believe in **traveling light**.

E. I got to the airport late and got
bumped!

F. I just arrived on the **red-eye** this
morning from New York.

G. Next time, I'm only bringing a
carry-on.

H. Now I'm **wired**!

I. I hope this **jet lag** doesn't last long!

J. I'm using a special **frequent flyer**
ticket.

K. She lives **way out in the boonies**!

L. Fortunately, they agreed to put me on
standby.

C. COMPLETE THE PHRASE *(Answers on p. 138)*

Complete the opening dialogue using the list below. Try not to look at the dialogue at the beginning of the lesson until you're done!

CD-A: TRACK 33

BARF	BOONIES
LAYOVER	BUMPED
EYE	CARRY-ON
LIGHT	WIRED
LAG	WIPED
FLYER	STANDBY

Karen is at the airport waiting for Steve to arrive.

Steve: I'm sorry we're so late. We had an unexpected two-hour _layover_ some place **way out in the** _boonies_ . You know, I almost missed the flight entirely because of all the traffic! So I arrived late and **got** _bumped_ . Luckily, they agreed to put me on _standby_ . All I had was a _carry-on_ , so it was easy.

Karen: It's a good thing you **travel** _light_ . Well, with the **jet** _lag_ , I imagine you're pretty _wiped_ **out**.

Steve: Actually, I'm pretty _wired_ after all that traveling. At least I got a free ticket for being a **frequent** _flyer_ !

Karen: So, how was it traveling on the **red-** _eye_ ?

Steve: It got a little bumpy for a while. Luckily, I never had to use the _barf_ **bag**!

LESSON 6 · AT A RESTAURANT

"Let's grab a bite!"

LET'S WARM UP!

MATCH THE PICTURES *(Answers on p. 138)*

As a fun way to get started, see if you can guess the meaning of the new slang words and expressions on the opposite page by using the pictures below and following the context of the sentences.

1. I eat too much. I need to **cut down**.
   ❏ eat less
   ❏ eat more

2. Let's order hamburgers and **a side of** fries?
   ❏ a small amount of
   ❏ an additional order of

3. I'm going to **skip** the salad. I've eaten enough vegetables today.
   ❏ omit
   ❏ add

4. Let's **go Dutch** today and just split the bill.
   ❏ pay separately
   ❏ get someone else to pay

5. I love desserts. I have a **sweet tooth**.
   ❏ dislike for sweets
   ❏ passion for sweets

6. You think you can eat all that?! **Your eyes are bigger than your stomach**!
   ❏ You always finish everything on your plate
   ❏ You believe you can eat more than you can

7. I'll finish this sandwich tomorrow. I can eat the **leftovers** for lunch.
   ❏ remaining food
   ❏ freshly prepared food

8. Leave your money at home. Lunch **is on me**.
   ❏ is going to be paid for by me
   ❏ is going to be made by me

9. I'm hungry. Let's **grab a bite** before the movie.
   ❏ visit the dentist
   ❏ get something to eat

10. Irene ate a box of chocolates today. She's a real **chocaholic**!
    ❏ chocolate hater
    ❏ chocolate lover

11. What a meal! I really **pigged out**!
    ❏ ate lightly
    ❏ ate in excess

12. I can't eat any more. I need a **doggie bag**.
    ❏ bag to carry food home
    ❏ bag of donuts

LET'S TALK!

A. DIALOGUE USING SLANG & IDIOMS

The words introduced on the first two pages are used in the following dialogue and illustrated in the long picture above. Can you understand the conversation and find the illustration that corresponds to the slang? *Note*: The translation of the words in boldface is on the right-hand page.

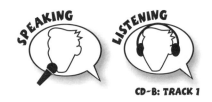

CD-B: TRACK 1

Cecily and Jim are **grabbing a bite**.

Cecily: I know we were going to **go Dutch** for lunch, but since today is your birthday, lunch **is on me**.

Jim: Well, I was planning on **cutting down**, but if you're paying, I'm going to **pig out**!

Cecily: Good! It's your birthday! Have whatever you want. I feel like having a big juicy hamburger and **a side of** fries. How about you?

Jim: I'll have the same. I think I'll also get an order of onion rings, potato salad, baked beans, cole slaw, and some biscuits. And to satisfy my **sweet tooth**, I'll get a slice of chocolate pie. You know what a **chocaholic** I am!

Cecily: Jim, **your eyes are bigger than your stomach**.

Jim: Maybe you're right. Okay. **Skip** the salad.

Cecily: I have a feeling you're going to need a **doggie bag** for all the **leftovers**. And I'm going to need to get a second job to pay for this lunch!

B. DIALOGUE TRANSLATED INTO STANDARD ENGLISH

LET'S SEE HOW MUCH YOU REMEMBER!
Just for fun, bounce around in random order to the words and expressions in boldface below. See if you can remember their slang equivalents without looking at the left-hand page!

Cecily and Jim are **getting something to eat**.

Cecily: I know we were going to **pay separately** for lunch, but since today is your birthday, **I'll pay for** lunch.

Jim: Well, I was planning on **dieting**, but if you're paying, I'm going to **eat in excess**!

Cecily: Good! It's your birthday! Have whatever you want. I feel like having a big juicy hamburger and **an extra order of** fries. How about you?

Jim: I'll have the same. I think I'll also get an order of onion rings, potato salad, baked beans, cole slaw, and some biscuits. And to satisfy my **passion for sweets**, I'll get a slice of chocolate pie. You know what a **chocolate lover** I am!

Cecily: Jim, **you believe you can eat more than you actually can**.

Jim: Maybe you're right. Okay. **Omit** the salad.

Cecily: I have a feeling you're going to need a **bag used to carry food home** for all the **excess food**. And I'm going to need to get a second job to pay for this lunch!

C. DIALOGUE USING "REAL SPEAK"

CD-B: TRACK 1

The dialogue below demonstrates how the slang conversation on the previous page would *really* be spoken by native speakers!

Cecily 'n Jim'er **grabbing a bite**.

Cecily: I know we w'r gonna **go Dutch** fer lunch, b't since taday's yer birthday, lunch **is on me**.

Jim: Well, I w'z planning on **cudding down**, b't if yer paying, I'm gonna **pig out**!

Cecily: Good! It's yer birthday! Have whadever ya want. I feel like having a big juicy burger an' **a side 'a** fries. How 'bout chu?

Jim: Ah'll have the same. In fact, I think ah'll also ged 'n order of onion rings, patado salad, s'm bake' beans, cole slaw, an' s'm biscuits. An' ta sadify my **sweet tooth**, ah'll ged a slice 'a choc'lit pie. Ya know whadda **chocaholic** I am!

Cecily: Jim, **yer eyes 'er bigger th'n yer stomach**.

Jim: Maybe yer right. Okay. **Skip** the salad.

Cecily: I have a feeling yer gonna need a **doggie bag** fer all the **leftovers**. An' I'm gonna need da ged a secon' job da pay fer this lunch!

KEY TO "REAL SPEAK"

GOING TO = GONNA

This is one of the most common reductions in American English and is sure to be heard when talking with just about any native speaker!

RULES

When "going to" is used to show future, it is often shortened (or *reduced*) to **gonna**.

HOW DOES IT WORK?

We're **going to** grab a bite. ↓ ↓ We're **going to** grab a bite.	In the phrase "going to," the hard sounds of "g" at the end of a word and "t" at the beginning of a word, disappear in everyday speech.
We're **goin o** grab a bite. ↓ ↓ We're **guhn uh** grab a bite.	Many vowel combinations (such as the "oi" in "going") and unstressed vowels (such as the "o" in "to") are commonly pronounced **uh**.
We're **gonna** grab a bite.	This shortened version of "going to" is so common in everyday speech that it is often seen written in magazines and newspapers to indicate spoken language.

BUT!

"Going to" is *never* shortened to **gonna** when it indicates going from one place to another!

INCORRECT	CORRECT
Are you **gonna** the meeting?	Are you **going to** the meeting?
I'm **gonna** the office tonight.	I'm **going to** the office tonight.
Everyone was **gonna** the restaurant.	Everyone was **going to** the restaurant.
Are you **gonna** the movies?	Are you **going to** the movies?
Why aren't they **gonna** the party with us?	Why aren't they **going to** the party with us?
She's **gonna** Paris today!	She's **going to** Paris today!

LET'S USE "REAL SPEAK!"

A. NOW YOU'RE GONNA DO A "GONNA" EXERCISE *(Answers on p. 138)*

Repeat the sentences replacing "going to" with "gonna."

1. I'm so hungry! I'm going to **pig out** tonight! ⁱᵍᵒⁿⁿᵃ

2. This restaurant serves such big portions. I'm ᵍᵒⁿⁿᵃ going to need a **doggie bag**.

3. I'm starting to get fat. I'm going to have to ᵍᵒⁿⁿᵃ **cut down** on desserts.

4. I'd like a hamburger but I'm going to **skip** ᵍᵒⁿⁿᵃ the fries.

5. I'm having lunch with Irene ᵍᵒⁿⁿᵃ today, but we're going to **go Dutch**.

6. If David is anything like his mother, he's going ᵍᵒⁿⁿᵃ to be a **chocaholic** when he grows up.

7. We have a lot of extra food from the party. Steve is going to take home the **leftovers**.

8. I'm hungry. I'm going to go **grab a bite**.

B. IS IT "GONNA" OR "GOING TO"? *(Answers on p. 139)*

Read the following paragraph and underline all the instances where "going to" can be reduced to "gonna." But be careful! There are two places where "going to" cannot change!

Janet and I are **going to** a great French restaurant tonight and we're **going to** pig out! I'm probably **going to** need a doggie bag because they serve so much food. After dinner, we're **going to** my mother's house and I'm **going to** bring her the leftovers. In fact, I'm **going to** order an extra chocolate dessert that I'm **going to** surprise her with. I know that's **going to** make her happy because she's a bigger chocaholic than I am!

LET'S LEARN!

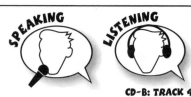

CD-B: TRACK 4

VOCABULARY

The following words and expressions were used in the previous dialogues. Let's take a closer look at what they mean.

chocaholic *n.* one who loves chocolate.

> **EXAMPLE:** My father is a **chocaholic**. He'll eat anything with chocolate on it!
>
> **TRANSLATION:** My father is a **lover of chocolate**. He'll eat anything with chocolate on it!
>
> **"REAL SPEAK":** My father's a **chocaholic**. He'll ead anything with choc'lit on it!
>
> *Note:* This is a play-on-words on the term *alcoholic,* meaning "a person addicted to alcohol." The suffix *-aholic* can be added to many words to suggest that the subject is addicted to something. For example: *food-aholic, shop-aholic, gym-aholic, etc.*

NOW YOU DO IT. COMPLETE THE PHRASE ALOUD:
I think Kim is a chocaholic because...

cut down on something (to) *v.* to decrease something (such as eating, spending, shopping, etc).

> **EXAMPLE:** I love desserts, but I'm trying **to cut down** because I've started to put on weight!
>
> **TRANSLATION:** I love desserts, but I'm trying **to eat less of them** because I've started to put on weight!
>
> **"REAL SPEAK":** I love desserts, bud I'm trying **ta cut down** 'cuz I've starded da pud on weight!
>
> *Variation:* **cut back on something (to)** *exp.*
> *Also:* **cut out something (to)** *exp.* to eliminate something completely.

NOW YOU DO IT. COMPLETE THE PHRASE ALOUD:
I'm trying to cut down on...

doggie bag *n.* a bag used to carry leftover food home from a restaurant.

> **EXAMPLE:** I can't finish all this food. I'm going to ask our waiter for a **doggie bag**.
>
> **TRANSLATION:** I can't finish all this food. I'm going to ask our waiter for a **bag to take this food home**.
>
> **"REAL SPEAK":** I can't finish all this food. I'm gonna ask 'ar waider fer a **doggie bag**.
>
> *Note:* This term was originally used to refer to a bag that people could use to take bones home from a restaurant to their dog or "*doggie*" (a child's term for "dog").

NOW YOU DO IT. COMPLETE THE PHRASE ALOUD:
I need a doggie bag to take home this...

Dutch (to go) *exp.* to pay individually.

EXAMPLE: Every time William and Steven eat at a restaurant, they **go Dutch**.

TRANSLATION: Every time William and Steven eat at a restaurant, they **pay individually**.

"REAL SPEAK": Ev'ry time William 'n Steven ead at a rest'rant, they **go Dutch**.

NOW YOU DO IT. COMPLETE THE PHRASE ALOUD:
David and I went Dutch to the...

eyes that are bigger than one's stomach (to have) *exp.* to think one can eat more than one actually can.

EXAMPLE: You're going to eat all that food? I have a feeling **your eyes are bigger than your stomach**.

TRANSLATION: You're going to eat all that food? I have a feeling **you think you can eat more than you can**.

"REAL SPEAK": Yer gonna ead all that food? I have a feeling **yer eyes 'er bigger th'n yer stomach**.

NOW YOU DO IT. COMPLETE THE PHRASE ALOUD:
My mom said my eyes are bigger than my stomach because...

grab a bite (to) *exp.* to get something to eat.

EXAMPLE: I'm starting to get hungry. Do you want to **grab a bite** somewhere?

TRANSLATION: I'm starting to get hungry. Do you want to **get something to eat** somewhere?

"REAL SPEAK": I'm starding da get hungry. Ya wanna **grab a bite** somewhere?

Variation: **grab a bite to eat (to)** *exp.*

NOW YOU DO IT. COMPLETE THE PHRASE ALOUD:
Yesterday I grabbed a bite at...

leftovers *n.* remaining food that couldn't be finished.

EXAMPLE: Do you want to come to my house for dinner? We have a lot of **leftovers** from the party last night.

TRANSLATION: Do you want to come to my house for dinner? We have a lot of **remaining food** from the party last night.

"REAL SPEAK": Ya wanna come ta my house fer dinner? We have a lod 'a **leftovers** fr'm the pardy las' night.

NOW YOU DO IT. COMPLETE THE PHRASE ALOUD:
My favorite leftovers are...

on someone (to be) *exp.* to be paid for by someone else.

EXAMPLE: Since you did such a big favor for me yesterday, **dinner is on me**.

TRANSLATION: Since you did such a big favor for me yesterday, **I'm paying for dinner**.

"REAL SPEAK": Since ya did such a big faver fer me yesderday, **dinner's on me**.

NOW YOU DO IT. COMPLETE THE PHRASE ALOUD:
In honor of your... lunch is on me.

pig out (to) *exp.* to eat in excess, to overeat, to eat like a pig.

EXAMPLE: I don't think I'm going to eat dinner tonight. I **pigged out** during lunch and I'm still full!

TRANSLATION: I don't think I'm going to eat dinner tonight. I **overate** during lunch and I'm still full!

"REAL SPEAK": I don' think I'm gonna eat dinner tanight. I **pigged out** during lunch 'n I'm still full!

Synonym: **pork out (to)** *exp.*

NOW YOU DO IT. COMPLETE THE PHRASE ALOUD:
The last time I pigged out was...

side of something (a) *n.* (used when ordering food) an extra order of something.

EXAMPLE: Since my hamburger doesn't come with anything extra, I'm going to get **a side of** cole slaw.

TRANSLATION: Since my hamburger doesn't come with anything extra, I'm going to get **an extra order of** cole slaw.

"REAL SPEAK": Since my burger doesn't come with anything extra, I'm gonna ged **a side 'a** cole slaw.

Note: Cole slaw (or slaw) is a popular salad made of shredded cabbage and mayonnaise.

NOW YOU DO IT. COMPLETE THE PHRASE ALOUD:
I'm so hungry that I'm going to order a side of...

skip something (to) *v.* to omit something from one's food order.

EXAMPLE: I'm going to **skip** the salad today and just have a sandwich and a drink.

TRANSLATION: I'm going to **decide against ordering** the salad today and just have a sandwich and a drink.

"REAL SPEAK": I'm gonna **skip** the salad taday 'n just have a san'wich 'n a drink.

NOW YOU DO IT. COMPLETE THE PHRASE ALOUD:
I think I'd better skip dessert tonight because after lunch I...

sweet tooth (to have a) *v.* to have a passion for sweets.

EXAMPLE:	Did you see all the candy Irene ate? She must really have a **sweet tooth**!
TRANSLATION:	Did you see all the candy Irene ate? She must really have a **passion for sweets**!
"REAL SPEAK":	Did'ja see all the candy Irene ate? She must really have a **sweet tooth**!

NOW YOU DO IT. COMPLETE THE PHRASE ALOUD:
I think... has a sweet tooth because yesterday I saw him/her eat a...

LET'S PRACTICE!

CD-B: TRACK 5

A. CHOOSE THE RIGHT WORD *(Answers on p. 139)*

Underline the appropriate word that best completes the phrase.

1. I'd love to go with you to the restaurant, but let's go (**French**, **Spanish**, **Dutch**✓).

2. I can't finish all this food. I think I'm going to need a (**kitty**, **birdie**, **doggie**✓) bag.

3. I'm starting to get fat! I'd better start to cut (**down**✓, **up**, **out**).

4. I'm hungry. Let's go grab a (**chew**, **bite**✓, **swallow**) before the movie.

5. I'm going to (**jump**, **hop**, **skip**✓) dessert. I'm trying to lose weight.

6. Did you see all the dessert Cecily ate? She must really have a sweet (**tooth**✓, **mouth**, **ear**).

7. Since today is your birthday, dinner is (**on**✓, **off**, **over**) me.

8. I'm starving! I'm really going to (**cow**, **giraffe**, **pig**✓) out during dinner!

9. Why did you order so much food? I think your (**ears**, **eyes**✓, **elbows**) are bigger than your stomach!

10. I'm going to order a (**top**, **bottom**, **side**✓) of French fries to go with my hamburger.

11. I think we bought too much food for the party. Look at all these left(**uppers**, **overs**✓, **downers**)!

12. No one loves (**chalk**, **chocolate**✓, **choking**) as much as my mother. She's such a chocaholic!

B. CROSSWORD PUZZLE *(Answers on p. 139)*

Fill in the crossword puzzle by choosing the correct word from the list below.

CD-B: TRACK 6

cutting	chocaholic	sweet
stomach	side	leftovers
on	Dutch	pig
skip	bag	bite

ACROSS

1. You want to order two hamburgers, French fries, salad, and dessert?! I think your eyes are bigger than your stomach

11. Steve has never offered to pay for my lunch even once. Every time we go out to eat, we always go Dutch

18. I'm hungry. We have a little extra time before the show starts. Let's grab a bite at that new restaurant that just opened yesterday.

19. Since today is your birthday, lunch is on me.

23. I have to start cut down or I'm going to get fat!

27. Why don't we order a side of spaghetti that we can share with our meal.

32. I'm going to skip dessert today. I couldn't eat another thing.

38. I couldn't possibly eat another bite. I'm going to ask the waiter for a doggie bag .

DOWN

1. For dessert I ate a big piece of chocolate cake, a slice of lemon pie, six chocolate chip cookies, and a brownie. I've always had a sweet tooth!

6. Tessa could easily eat an entire chocolate cake all by herself. Everyone knows she's a real chocaholic

17. I think I bought too much food for the party. We'll never be able to eat all this food. I suppose we can always eat the leftover tomorrow.

33. Yesterday for dinner, I went to an all-you-can-eat restaurant. You should have seem me pig out!

C. MATCH THE COLUMN *(Answers on p. 140)*

Match the words in boldface with the definition in the right column. Write the letter of the definition in the box.

CD-B: TRACK 7

[F] 1. Let's go **grab a bite** before the movie starts. I know a great restaurant just around the corner.

A. eating less

[B] 2. I don't usually eat desserts. I guess I never really developed much of a **sweet tooth**.

B. passion for sweets

[I] 3. I'm tired of always paying for Bill every time we go out for dinner. Next time, I want to **go Dutch**.

C. omit

[A] 4. If you don't start **cutting down**, you're going to gain weight.

D. eat in excess

[J] 5. I couldn't possibly eat another bite. I'm so full! I'd better ask the waiter for a **doggie bag**.

E. chocolate lover

[D] 6. Look at that beautiful buffet. I've never seen so much food! Let's go **pig out**.

F. get something to eat

[H] 7. Thank you for treating me to lunch yesterday. Let's go out to dinner today. **It's on me**.

G. the remaining food that couldn't be finished

[C] 8. I'm going to **skip** the salad tonight since I just had one during lunch.

H. I'll treat

[K] 9. If you're still hungry, you could always order **a side of** bread rolls or a salad.

I. pay individually

[G] 10. That was such a delicious meal, but there's so much food we didn't even touch. Well, I guess we can always have **leftovers** tomorrow.

J. bag used to carry remaining food home from a restaurant

[L] 11. Why did you take such a huge piece of pie? You'll never be able to finish that. I think **your eyes are bigger than your stomach**.

K. an extra order of

[E] 12. I think Joe is a **chocaholic**. He just ate an entire chocolate cake and two chocolate ice cream cones!

L. you believe you can eat more than you actually can

LET'S REVIEW!

THE GOOD, THE BAD, AND THE... *(Answers on p. 140)*

There were several slang terms and idioms in the first three lessons that were used to describe something either very good or very bad. Write the number of the slang term or idiom in Column A next to its matching picture in Column B as well as next to the matching definition in Column C.

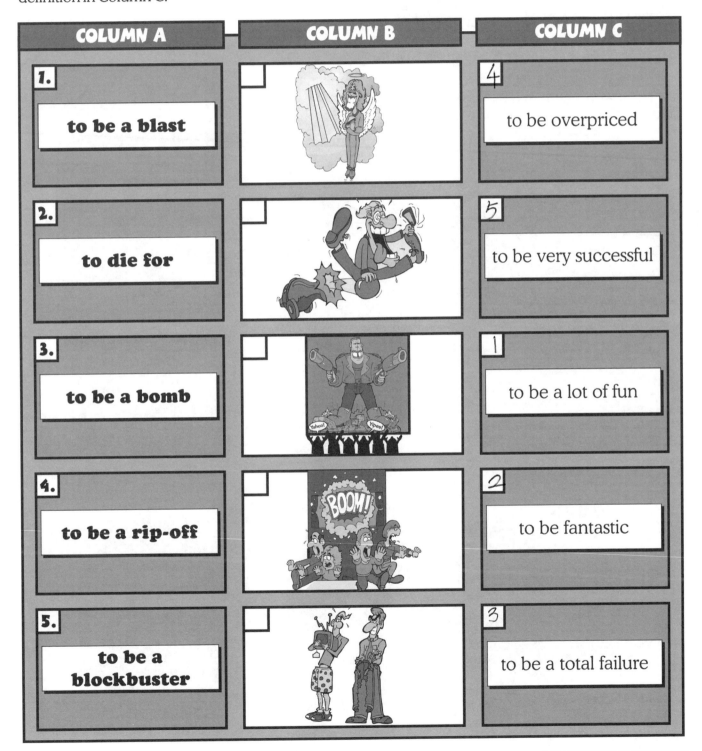

COLUMN A	COLUMN B	COLUMN C
1. to be a blast		**4** to be overpriced
2. to die for		**5** to be very successful
3. to be a bomb		**1** to be a lot of fun
4. to be a rip-off		**2** to be fantastic
5. to be a blockbuster		**3** to be a total failure

LESSON 7 ON THE ROAD

"Let's go for a spin!"

LET'S WARM UP!

MATCH THE PICTURES (Answers on p. 141)

As a fun way to get started, see if you can guess the meaning of the new slang words and expressions on the opposite page by using the pictures below and following the context of the sentences.

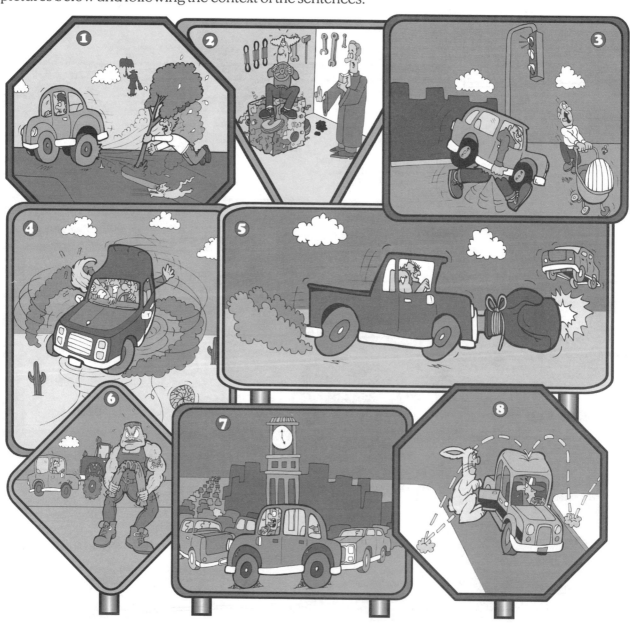

1. I drove my car over a nail and got a **blowout**.
   - ☐ flat tire
   - ☐ scratch on my car

2. My car was **totaled** in an accident. Now I have to buy a new one.
   - ☐ destroyed
   - ☐ damaged slightly

3. Yesterday a driver **ran a light** and almost hit me!
   - ☐ crashed into a light post
   - ☐ drove through a red light

4. Would you like to go for a **spin** in my new car?
   - ☐ drive
   - ☐ walk

5. I'm going to be late for work! I'd better **punch it**!
   - ☐ accelerate suddenly
   - ☐ stop suddenly

6. I was in a **fender-bender** today. The car repairs shouldn't cost very much.
   - ☐ minor car accident
   - ☐ major car accident

7. Yesterday, it took me an hour to drive home during **rush hour**, and I only live a mile away!
   - ☐ the time when everyone is driving on the road
   - ☐ the time when no one is driving on the road

8. I'll be glad to drive you to the market. **Hop in**!
   - ☐ start jumping
   - ☐ get in

9. Bob got **hauled in** for speeding! He may have to spend the night in jail!
   - ☐ an award
   - ☐ arrested

10. The **bumper-to-bumper traffic** made me late!
   - ☐ light traffic
   - ☐ heavy traffic

11. The **cop** just arrested that man for bank robbery!
   - ☐ fire fighter
   - ☐ police officer

12. I ruined my tires when I drove over those **pot holes**.
   - ☐ rocks in the street
   - ☐ deep holes in the street

13. I have to take the bus until my **clunker** gets fixed.
   - ☐ old bicycle
   - ☐ old car

14. I don't drive with Dan because he has a **lead foot**!
   - ☐ broken foot
   - ☐ tendency to drive very fast

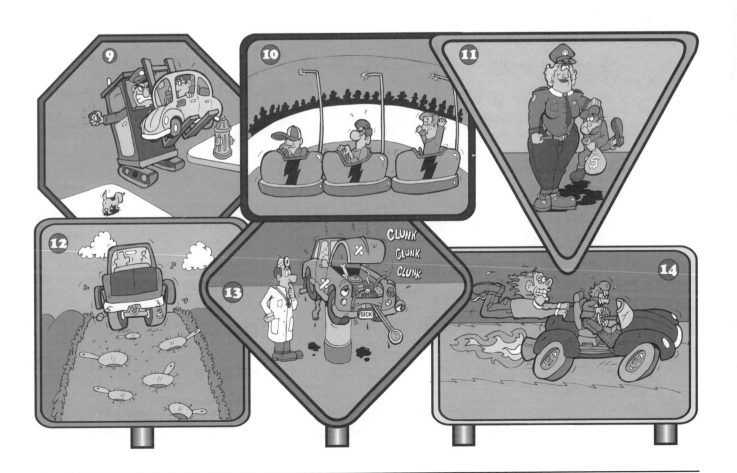

LET'S TALK!

A. DIALOGUE USING SLANG & IDIOMS

The words introduced on the first two pages are used in the following dialogue and illustrated in the long picture above. Can you understand the conversation and find the illustration that corresponds to the slang? *Note:* The translation of the words in boldface is on the right-hand page.

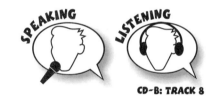

CD-B: TRACK 8

John is showing Mark his new car.

Mark: Is this your new car? It's beautiful!

John: Thanks. It sure is a step up from the **clunker** I used to have. **Hop in** and I'll take you for a **spin**.

Mark: Just be careful. I know about that **lead foot** of yours. You don't want to get into a **fender-bender**! And you definitely don't want to get **hauled in** by a **cop** for speeding or **running a light**.

John: Don't worry. I promise I'm not going to **total my car** or get arrested my first day having a new car.

Mark: Okay, but be careful. The road to Nancy's house is full of **pot holes** and you don't want to get a **blowout**.

John: Don't worry! I'll take it slowly. Besides, since this is **rush hour**, we're not going to be able to go very fast with all the **bumper-to-bumper traffic**! But once it clears up, I'm going to **punch it**!

B. DIALOGUE TRANSLATED INTO STANDARD ENGLISH

LET'S SEE HOW MUCH YOU REMEMBER!
Just for fun, bounce around in random order to the words and expressions in boldface below. See if you can remember their slang equivalents without looking at the left-hand page!

John is showing Mark his new car.

Mark: Is this your new car? It's beautiful!

John: Thanks. It sure is a step up from the **old car** I used to have. **Get in** and I'll take you for a **drive**.

Mark: Just be careful. I know about your **tendency to drive fast**. You don't want to get into a **car accident**! And you definitely don't want to get **arrested** by a **police officer** for speeding or **driving through a red light**.

John: Don't worry. I promise I'm not going to **destroy my car** or get arrested my first day having a new car.

Mark: Okay, but be careful. The road to Nancy's house is full of **deep holes** and you don't want to get a **flat tire**.

John: Don't worry! I'll take it slowly. Besides, since this is **the time when most of the cars are on the road**, we're not going to be able to go very fast with all the **heavy traffic**! But once it clears up, I'm going to **accelerate quickly**!

C. DIALOGUE USING "REAL SPEAK"

The dialogue below demonstrates how the slang conversation on the previous page would *really* be spoken by native speakers!

CD-B: TRACK 8

John's showing Mark 'is new car.

Mark: Is this yer new car? It's beaudiful!

John: Thanks. It's sher a step up fr'm the **clunker** I usta have. **Hop in** 'n ah'll take ya fer a **spin**.

Mark: Jus' be careful. I know about cher **lead foot**. Ya don't wanna ged into a **fender-bender**! And ya definitely don't wanna get **hauled in** by a **cop** fer speeding 'r **running a light**.

John: Don't worry. I promise I'm not gonna **todal my car** 'r ged arrested my firs' day having a new car.

Mark: Okay, b't be careful. The road ta Nancy's house is full 'a **pot holes** 'n ya don't wanna ged a **blowout**.

John: Don't worry! Ah'll take it slowly. Besides, since this is **rush hour**, w'r not gonna be able da go very fast with all the **bumper-da-bumper traffic**! B't once it clears up, I'm gonna **punch it**!

KEY TO "REAL SPEAK"
WANT TO = WANNA

In the above dialogue using "real speak," "want to" became **wanna**. This is a very informal style of speech and can certainly be used in business as well.

RULES

In everyday conversation, "want to" is commonly reduced to **wanna**, and "wants to" is commonly reduced to **wansta**. Personal pronouns *I, you, we* and *they* use **wanna**; *he* and *she* use **wansta**, as demonstrated below.

HOW DOES IT WORK?

I ***want to*** go for a spin.
I ***wanXXo*** go for a spin.

> In the phrase "want to," the sound of both *t*'s disappears in everyday speech.

I ***wan o*** go for a spin.
I ***wan uh*** go for a spin.

> All unstressed vowels (such as the **o** in "to" of "want to") are commonly pronounced **uh**.

I ***wanna*** go for a spin.

> This shortened version of "want to" is so common in everyday speech that it is often seen written in magazines and newspapers to indicate spoken language.

WANNA / WANSTA CHART

I	I **want to** go for a spin.	➤	I **wanna** go for a spin.
you	Do you **want to** hop in and go?	➤	Do you **wanna** hop in and go?
we	We **want to** miss rush hour.	➤	We **wanna** miss rush hour.
they	They **want to** sell their old clunker.	➤	They **wanna** sell their old clunker.
he	He **wants to** avoid the pot holes.	➤	He **wansta** avoid the pot holes.
she	She **wants to** grab a cab.	➤	She **wansta** grab a cab.

LET'S USE "REAL SPEAK!"

A. WANNA OR WANSTA *(Answers on p. 141)*

Answer the question in Column A aloud using the words in Column B. Make sure to use "wanna" or "wansta" in your answers.

SPEAKING

CD-B: TRACK 9

COLUMN A	COLUMN B
1. Do you want to take in a movie tonight?	[Yes] [see] [comedy]
2. What does your brother want to do tonight?	[He] [pig out] [pizza]
3. What do your friends want to order for dinner?	[Everybody] [hamburgers] [side of fries]
4. Does Steve want to take home the leftovers?	[Yes] [he] [doggie bag]
5. Do you want to take a drive in my new car?	[Yes] [spin] [beach]
6. Where does your mother want to go for dinner?	[She] [eat] [French restaurant]
7. Does anybody want to play cards tonight?	[Nobody] [play cards] [watch TV]
8. Does the cat want to go outside?	[No] [sleep] [sofa]

LET'S LEARN!

VOCABULARY

The following words and expressions were used in the previous dialogues. Let's take a closer look at what they mean.

blowout *n.* (said because the air "blows out" of the tire) a punctured tire.

EXAMPLE:	I was late to work because I got a **blowout** on the highway this morning.
TRANSLATION:	I was late to work because I got a **punctured tire** on the highway this morning.
"REAL SPEAK":	I w'z late ta work 'cuz I god a **blowoud** on the highway this morning.
Synonym:	**flat** *n.* (short for: *flat tire*).

NOW YOU DO IT. COMPLETE THE PHRASE ALOUD:

My car got a blowout on my way to...

bumper-to-bumper traffic *exp.* traffic that is so heavy that there is no room between cars.

EXAMPLE:	It took me two hours to get home because of all the **bumper-to-bumper traffic** and I only live a few miles from work!
TRANSLATION:	It took me two hours to get home because of all the **heavy traffic** and I only live a few miles from work!
"REAL SPEAK":	It took me two hours ta get home because of all the **bumper-da-bumper traffic** an' I only live a few miles fr'm work!

NOW YOU DO IT. COMPLETE THE PHRASE ALOUD:

The road to ...is known for having a lot of bumper-to-bumper traffic.

clunker *n.* an old car in poor condition.

EXAMPLE:	I finally sold my old **clunker** and bought a new Mercedes Benz!
TRANSLATION:	I finally sold my old **worn out car** and bought a new Mercedes Benz!
"REAL SPEAK":	I fin'lly sold my old **clunker** 'n bod a new Mercedes Benz!
Synonym:	**jalopy** *n.*

NOW YOU DO IT. COMPLETE THE PHRASE ALOUD:

The last clunker I owned was a...

cop *n.* police officer (originally called a *copper*).

EXAMPLE:	Be careful not to speed on this street. I just saw a **cop**.
TRANSLATION:	Be careful not to speed on this street. I just saw a **police officer**.
"REAL SPEAK":	Be careful not ta speed on this street. I jus' saw a **cop**.
Note:	This popular term (used even among police officers) came from the days of gangsters when police officers were known for wearing a copper badge.

NOW YOU DO IT. COMPLETE THE PHRASE ALOUD:

The job of a cop is to...

fender-bender *n.* a minor car accident.

EXAMPLE:	I got into a car accident this morning, but don't worry. It was just a **fender-bender**.
TRANSLATION:	I got into a car accident this morning, but don't worry. It was just a **minor accident**.
"REAL SPEAK":	I god into a car accident this morning, b't don't worry. It w'z just a **fender-bender**.

NOW YOU DO IT. COMPLETE THE PHRASE ALOUD:

The last time I saw a fender-bender was...

hauled in (to get) *exp.* to get taken to the police station.

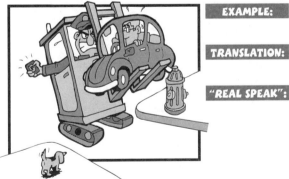

EXAMPLE:	Did you hear the news? Jim got **hauled in** for drunk driving!
TRANSLATION:	Did you hear the news? Jim got **taken to the police station** for drunk driving!
"REAL SPEAK":	Did'ja hear the news? Jim got **hauled in** fer drunk driving!

NOW YOU DO IT. COMPLETE THE PHRASE ALOUD:

I've never been hauled in for...

hop in (to) *v.* to get into a car.

EXAMPLE:	I'd be happy to drive you to the grocery store this morning. **Hop in**!
TRANSLATION:	I'd be happy to drive you to the grocery store this morning. **Get in the car**!
"REAL SPEAK":	I'd be happy da drive you da the groc'ry store this morning. **Hop in**!

NOW YOU DO IT. COMPLETE THE PHRASE ALOUD:

Hop in! I'd be glad to drive you to...

lead foot (to have a) *exp.* said of a driver who has a tendency to drive faster than the speed limit (as if his/her foot were made of lead, causing the car's gas pedal to be pressed too far down).

EXAMPLE: My brother got his third speeding ticket in two weeks! My father is always yelling at him about his **lead foot**.

TRANSLATION: My brother got his third speeding ticket in two weeks! My father is always yelling at him about his **tendency to drive too fast**.

"REAL SPEAK": My brother god 'is third speeding ticket 'n two weeks! My dad's always yelling ad 'im aboud 'is **lead foot**.

NOW YOU DO IT. COMPLETE THE PHRASE ALOUD:
My (family member or friend) has a lead foot!

pot hole *n.* a large hole in the street resembling the size and depth of a kitchen pot.

EXAMPLE: Unfortunately, the city doesn't have enough money to fix all the **pot holes**.

TRANSLATION: Unfortunately, the city doesn't have enough money to fix all the **holes in the street**.

"REAL SPEAK": Unfortunately, the cidy doesn' have anuf money da fix all the **pot holes**.

NOW YOU DO IT. COMPLETE THE PHRASE ALOUD:
[Street name] has a lot of pot holes!

punch it (to) *exp.* to press the accelerator pedal down suddenly.

EXAMPLE: **Punch it**! We only have five minutes before the movie starts!

TRANSLATION: **Accelerate immediately**! We only have five minutes before the movie starts!

"REAL SPEAK": **Punch it**! We only have five minutes b'fore the movie starts!

NOW YOU DO IT. COMPLETE THE PHRASE ALOUD:
We're late for.... Punch it!

run a light (to) *exp.* to go through a traffic signal during a red light.

EXAMPLE: Did you see that?! That guy **ran the light** and almost hit us!

TRANSLATION: Did you see that?! That guy **went through the traffic signal during a red light** and almost hit us!

"REAL SPEAK": Did'ja see that?! That guy **ran the light** 'n almost hid us!

NOW YOU DO IT. COMPLETE THE PHRASE ALOUD:
The danger in running a red light is...

rush hour *n.* the time when most drivers are on the road at the same time (usually at the opening or close of business).

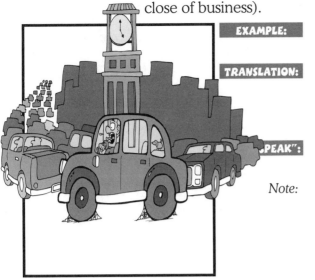

EXAMPLE: Let's meet for dinner tonight, but let's make it around seven o'clock. I don't want to drive during **rush hour**.

TRANSLATION: Let's meet for dinner tonight, but let's make it around seven o'clock. I don't want to drive during **the time when most drivers are on the road at the same time**.

"REAL SPEAK": Let's meet fer dinner danight, b't let's make id aroun' seven a'clock. I don't wanna drive during **rush hour**.

Note: This term is still commonly used although it's no longer accurate, since in most big cities **rush hour** actually lasts for *several* hours!

NOW YOU DO IT. COMPLETE THE PHRASE ALOUD:
During rush hour, it takes me ...hours to get to...

spin (to take a) *exp.* to take a short drive with no particular destination.

EXAMPLE: It's such a beautiful day! Why don't we **take a spin** in my new car?

TRANSLATION: It's such a beautiful day! Why don't we **take a relaxing drive** in my new car?

"REAL SPEAK": It's such a beaudif'l day! Why don' we **take a spin** 'n my new car?

Variation: **spin (to go for a)** *exp.*

NOW YOU DO IT. COMPLETE THE PHRASE ALOUD:
If I had a Porsche, I'd ask ...if he/she wanted to take a spin with me!

total a car (to) *exp.* to completely destroy a car in an accident.

EXAMPLE: Did you hear the news? Pat **totaled his car** in an accident last night! Luckily, no one was hurt.

TRANSLATION: Did you hear the news? Pat **destroyed his car** in an accident last night! Luckily, no one was hurt.

"REAL SPEAK": Did'ja hear the news? Pat **todaled 'is car** in 'n accident las' night! Luckily, no one w'z hurt.

NOW YOU DO IT. COMPLETE THE PHRASE ALOUD:
If I total my father's new car, he will...

LET'S PRACTICE!

CD-B: TRACK 11

A. CORRECT OR INCORRECT (Answers on p. 141)

Decide whether or not the words in boldface have been used correctly or incorrectly by checking the appropriate box.

1. George just bought a brand new **clunker**. It's beautiful!
   ☐ CORRECT   ☒ INCORRECT

2. You're driving too fast! **Punch it**!
   ☐ CORRECT   ☒ INCORRECT

3. Becky always drives too fast. She has a real **lead foot**.
   ☒ CORRECT   ☐ INCORRECT

4. I made it home easily because there was **bumper-to-bumper traffic** the entire way.
   ☐ CORRECT   ☒ INCORRECT

5. The roads in the city are in perfect condition. They all have lots of **pot holes**.
   ☐ CORRECT   ☒ INCORRECT

6. Do you need a ride to the market? **Hop in**!
   ☒ CORRECT   ☐ INCORRECT

7. I feel like taking a walk today. Let's go for a **spin**.
   ☐ CORRECT   ☒ INCORRECT

8. Let's try to drive out of the city around **rush hour**. That's when there won't be many cars on the road.
   ☐ CORRECT   ☒ INCORRECT

9. On the way to my mother's house, I drove over a nail and got a **blowout**.
   ☒ CORRECT   ☐ INCORRECT

10. I heard you got into an accident yesterday and **totaled** your car! Were you hurt? Is your car really ruined?
    ☒ CORRECT   ☐ INCORRECT

11. That driver almost **ran the light** and hit me!
    ☒ CORRECT   ☐ INCORRECT

12. My sister wants to be a **cop** because she loves fighting fires.
    ☐ CORRECT   ☒ INCORRECT

CD-B: TRACK 12

B. BLANK-BLANK *(Answers on p. 141)*

Fill in the blank with the correct word(s) from Column B.

COLUMN A	COLUMN B
1. It took me an hour to drive home because of all the *bumper-to-bumper traffic*.	**cop**
2. It's such a beautiful day. Let's put the top down and *go for a spin* in my new sports car.	**go for a spin**
3. That was really close! That driver didn't stop! He *ran the light* and almost hit us!	**totaled**
4. You drive too fast! You're just like your father. You have a *lead foot*!	**punch it**
5. We have to drive to the hospital fast. The contractions are coming every minute! *punch it*!!	**pot holes**
6. The car wasn't damaged too badly in the accident. It was just a little *fender-bender*.	**ran a light**
7. I'm going to the market, too. *Hop in*. I'd be happy to give you a ride there.	**hauled in**
8. It looks like I'm going to have to buy a new car after the accident. My poor car was *totaled*.	**fender-bender**
9. When are you going to get rid of that old *clunker* and buy yourself a new car?	**clunker**
10. I had to buy a new tire this morning because I got a *blowout* on the way to work.	**blowout**
11. My sister is a *cop*. Last week, she arrested two robbers!	**bumper-to-bumper traffic**
12. Look at all the cars on the road! I hate driving during *rush hour*!	**rush hour**
13. They really should fix these roads. They're so bumpy because of all the *pot holes*.	**hop in**
14. Did you hear the news? Rob got *hauled in* for drunk driving!!	**lead foot**

C. TRUE OR FALSE (Answers on p. 142)

CD-B: TRACK 13

Decide whether or not the definition of the word in boldface is true or false by checking an "X" in the correct box.

1. **cop** n. police officer (originally called a *copper* because of the copper badge).
☒ TRUE ☐ FALSE

2. **to hop in** v. to go through a red light.
☐ TRUE ☒ FALSE

3. **to punch it** exp. to get into a fight with a cop.
☐ TRUE ☒ FALSE

4. **to have a lead foot** exp. said of someone who has a tendency to drive fast (as if his/her foot were made of lead).
☒ TRUE ☐ FALSE

5. **blowout** n. a punctured tire.
☒ TRUE ☐ FALSE

6. **clunker** n. a brand new car.
☐ TRUE ☒ FALSE

7. **bumper-to-bumper traffic** exp. traffic that is so heavy that there is no room between cars.
☒ TRUE ☐ FALSE

8. **rush hour** n. a time when there are few cars on the road.
☐ TRUE ☒ FALSE

9. **to total a car** exp. to completely destroy a car in an accident.
☒ TRUE ☐ FALSE

10. **pot hole** n. a large hole in the street the size and depth of a kitchen pot.
☒ TRUE ☐ FALSE

11. **to run a light** exp. to drive with the headlights on.
☐ TRUE ☒ FALSE

12. **to take a spin** exp. to take a short drive with no particular destination.
☒ TRUE ☐ FALSE

13. **to get hauled in** exp. to get taken to the police station.
☒ TRUE ☐ FALSE

14. **fender-bender** n. a quick ride in the car.
☐ TRUE ☒ FALSE

LET'S REVIEW!

IN OTHER WORDS... SYNONYMS! *(Answers on p. 142)*

In the vocabulary section of previous lessons, you may have noticed that there were synonyms offered for many of the slang terms and idioms you have learned. Write the number of the picture from Column A next to its matching synonym in Column B.

COLUMN A

1.
to get on someone's case

2.
to put someone on

3.
to ring up

4.
blockbuster

5.
to have a blast

6.
to soak up some sun

7.
way out in the boonies

8.
to get a grip

9.
to be wired

10.
what's up with...?

11.
to pig out

12.
to pick up something

COLUMN B

3	to check out
9	to be buzzed
12	to grab something
1	to get on someone
7	way out in the boondocks
11	to pork out
4	smash hit
10	what's the deal with...?
2	to yank someone's chain
8	to pull oneself together
6	to have a ball
6	to soak up some rays

LESSON 8 AT SCHOOL

"I had to pull an all-nighter!"

LET'S WARM UP!

MATCH THE PICTURES *(Answers on p. 142)*

As a fun way to get started, see if you can guess the meaning of the new slang words and expressions on the opposite page by using the pictures below and following the context of the sentences.

1. I Tony **cut class** yesterday and went to the movies instead.

2. B My **psych** teacher is strange. I think she's neurotic!

3. E I'm so excited! I **aced** the test!

4. J I **pulled an all-nighter** studying! I'm exhausted.

5. D The teacher surprised us all by giving us a **pop quiz**!

6. N This class is too hard. I think I'm going to **drop it**.

7. C My sister always gets **straight A's** without even studying!

8. H If I don't pass the **final**, I'm going to be in big trouble!

9. G I **blew** my test. I'm studying harder next time!

10. L What a **killer** test! It was really hard!

11. A Paul **flunked** the course because he never studies.

12. M I missed the test because I was sick. I hope the teacher is giving a **make-up**.

13. K You forgot about the test tomorrow? You'd better **cram** for it!

14. F I passed the **mid-term**! My parents will be so happy!

A. failed

B. psychology

C. perfect grades

D. surprise test

E. did extremely well on

F. middle-of-term examination

G. did extremely poorly

H. end-of-term examination

I. didn't attend class

J. stayed up all night

K. study hard in a short period of time

L. very difficult

M. second chance at taking the test

N. remove the class from my schedule

LET'S TALK!

A. DIALOGUE USING SLANG & IDIOMS

The words introduced on the first two pages are used in the following dialogue and illustrated in the long picture above. Can you understand the conversation and find the illustration that corresponds to the slang? *Note*: The translation of the words in boldface is on the right-hand page.

CD-B: TRACK 14

Lee and David are talking about Eric.

David: I just heard Eric **flunked** our **psych** class! Is that true?

Lee: Yeah, I can't believe it. It's never happened to him before! He always gets **straight A's** on the **pop quizzes** and he even **aced** the **mid-term**. How could he possibly **blow** the **final**?

David: That's because he started to **cut class** all the time and stopped studying. I passed it because I **pulled an all nighter** trying to **cram** for it.

Lee: I've never taken such a **killer** test in my life. Unfortunately for Eric, the professor isn't allowing him to take a **make-up**.

David: He should have **dropped the class** when he had the chance!

B. DIALOGUE TRANSLATED INTO STANDARD ENGLISH

LET'S SEE HOW MUCH YOU REMEMBER!
Just for fun, bounce around in random order to the words and expressions in boldface below. See if you can remember their slang equivalents without looking at the left-hand page!

Lee and David are talking about Eric.

David: I just heard Eric **failed** our **psychology** class! Is that true?

Lee: Yeah, I can't believe it. It's never happened to him before! He always gets **perfect grades** on the **surprise tests** and he even **did extremely well on** the **mid-term examination**. How could he possibly **do extremely poorly on** the **final examination**?

David: That's because he started to **miss class intentionally** all the time and stopped studying. I passed it because I **stayed up all night** trying to **study hard** for it.

Lee: I've never taken such a **difficult** test in my life. Unfortunately for Eric, the professor isn't allowing him to take a **re-test**.

David: He should have **removed the class from his schedule** when he had the chance!

C. DIALOGUE USING "REAL SPEAK"

The dialogue below demonstrates how the slang conversation on the previous page would *really* be spoken by native speakers!

CD-B: TRACK 14

Lee 'n David 'er talking aboud Eric.

David: I just heard thad Eric **flunked** 'ar **psych** class! Izat true?

Lee: Yeah, I can't b'lieve it. It's never happen' to 'im b'fore! He always gets **straid A's** on the **pop quizzes** an' 'e even **aced** the **mid-term**. How could 'e possibly **blow** the **final**?

David: That's 'cuz 'e starded da **cut class** all the time 'n stopped studying. I passed it 'cuz I **pulled 'n all-nider** trying da **cram** for it.

Lee: I've never taken such a **killer** test in my life. Unfortunately fer Eric, the prafesser isn' allowing 'im ta take a **make-up**.

David: He should 'a **dropped the class** when 'e had the chance!

KEY TO "REAL SPEAK"

HE = 'E
HIM = 'IM
HIS = 'IS
HER = 'ER
THEM = 'EM

The disappearing "h" in these pronouns is one of the most common reductions in English. It is used by absolutely everyone!

RULES

The "h" often disappears from the pronouns "he," "him," "his," and "her" when they are not stressed in the sentence. However, the "h" <u>is</u> always pronounced when the pronoun is either stressed, begins the sentence, or follows a pause or comma.

Additionally, the "th" often disappears from the pronoun "them" when it is not stressed in the sentence. However, when "them" <u>is</u> stressed, the "th" is always pronounced. Note that the "real speak" pronunciation of "them" (***'em***) and "him" (***'im***) sounds the same. The distinction is made based on the context!

HOW DOES IT WORK?

I think **'e** flunked biology class.
I told **'im** he'd better cram for the test.
I hope Steve gets a good grade on **'is** final!
Kori thinks **'er** psych teacher is crazy.
Pop quizzes...I hate **'em**!

} In these examples, the "h" (or "th") is silent because *he, him, his, her,* and *them* are not stressed.

Every time I see David, **he** says hello to me.
Don't tell me you're upset. Tell **him**.
That's not my pencil. It's **his**.
You invited **her** to your party?
I wasn't talking to you. I was talking to **them**.
He left for college yesterday.
Her cat ruined all the furniture.

} In these examples, the "h" (or "th") <u>is</u> pronounced because the pronoun is either stressed, begins the sentence, or follows a pause or comma.

LET'S USE "REAL SPEAK!"

A. CHANGE 'EM TO REAL SPEAK *(Answers on p. 142)*

Fill in each box with the real speak version of **he ('e)**, **him ('im)**, **his ('is)**, **her ('er)**, or **them ('em)** when appropriate. But be careful! In some cases, there is no change! Most important, practice speaking the paragraph in real speak using your answers.

CD-B: TRACK 15

Last night I babysat my niece and nephew. You should have seen them ['em] . They're so cute!

Tessa is eight years old and her ['er] eyes look just like her ['er] mother's. When you look at

them ['em] in the sunlight, they look very dark blue. Her [Her] favorite food is ice cream and

her ['er] favorite color is red. Her [her] brother Nicholas just had his ['is] fifth birthday.

Everyone thinks he ['e] looks just like his ['is] father but he [he] thinks he [he] looks like

his ['is] grandfather. Frankly, whenever I see him ['im] smile, I think he [he] looks just like me!

After all, I'm his ['is] uncle! Both of them ['em] love to read. Yesterday, Tessa read a story to

her ['er] mother and Nicholas read one to his ['is] father. I'm glad they live so close. It's so

much fun watching them ['em] grow up!

LET'S LEARN!

CD-B: TRACK 16

VOCABULARY

The following words and expressions were used in the previous dialogues. Let's take a closer look at what they mean.

ace a test (to) *exp.* to do extremely well on a test.

EXAMPLE:	I studied for weeks and weeks. I just know I'm going to **ace the test**!
TRANSLATION:	I studied for weeks and weeks. I just know I'm going to **do extremely well on the test**!
"REAL SPEAK":	I studied fer weeks 'n weeks. I jus' know I'm gonna **ace the test**!

NOW YOU DO IT:
(Use "ace the test" in a sentence)

blow a test (to) *exp.* to do extremely poorly on a test.

EXAMPLE:	Steve **blew the test** in algebra. I always thought he loved math!
TRANSLATION:	Steve **did extremely poorly on the test** in algebra. I always thought he loved math!
"REAL SPEAK":	Steve **blew the test** 'n algebra. I always thod 'e loved math!

NOW YOU DO IT:
(Use "blow the test" in a sentence)

cram (to) *v.* to study very hard in a short period of time.

EXAMPLE:	I should have been studying all week. Now I have to stay up and **cram** for this test tomorrow morning!
TRANSLATION:	I should have been studying all week. Now I have to stay up and **study very hard in a short period of time** for this test tomorrow morning!
"REAL SPEAK":	I should'ev been studying all week. Now I hafta stay up 'n **cram** fer this tes' tamorrow morning!

NOW YOU DO IT:
(Use "cram" in a sentence)

cut class (to) *exp.* to miss class intentionally.

EXAMPLE: I don't feel like going to school today. Let's **cut class** and go to the movies.

TRANSLATION: I don't feel like going to school today. Let's **miss class intentionally** and go to the movies.

"REAL SPEAK": I don' feel like going ta school taday. Let's **cut class** 'n go da the movies.

NOW YOU DO IT:

(Use "cut class" in a sentence)

drop a class (to) *exp.* to remove a class from one's schedule.

EXAMPLE: You're taking eight classes this term? If you want any free time, you're going to have to **drop a class**… maybe two!

TRANSLATION: You're taking eight classes this term? If you want any free time, you're going to have to **remove a class from your schedule**… maybe two!

"REAL SPEAK": Yer taking eight classes this term? If ya wan' any free time, yer gonna hafta **drop a class**… maybe two!

NOW YOU DO IT:

(Use "drop a class" in a sentence)

final *n.* the final test which covers everything learned during the school term.

EXAMPLE: I need to study all week. If I don't pass the **final**, I won't be able to graduate!

TRANSLATION: I need to study all week. If I don't pass the **final test covering everything we learned**, I won't be able to graduate!

"REAL SPEAK": I need da study all week. If I don't pass the **final**, I won't be able da graduate!

NOW YOU DO IT:

(Use "final" in a sentence)

flunk (to) *v.* to fail a test or a subject.

EXAMPLE: I studied all night for this test! How could I have possibly **flunked**?

TRANSLATION: I studied all night for this test! How could I have possibly **failed**?

"REAL SPEAK": I studied all night fer this test! How could I'ev possibly **flunked**?

NOW YOU DO IT:

(Use "flunk" in a sentence)

killer *adj.* • **1.** extremely difficult • **2.** terrific.

EXAMPLE 1:	That was a **killer** test! I hope I didn't blow it!
TRANSLATION:	That was a **really difficult** test! I hope I didn't blow it!
"REAL SPEAK":	That w'z a **killer** test! I hope I didn't blow it!
EXAMPLE 2:	That's a **killer** dress! Where did you buy it?
TRANSLATION:	That's a **terrific** dress! Where did you buy it?
"REAL SPEAK":	That's a **killer** dress! Where'd 'ja buy it?
Note:	The difference between definitions **1.** and **2.** simply depends on the context.

NOW YOU DO IT:
(Use "killer" in a sentence)

make-up [or] **make-up test** *n.* a test that can be taken again at a later time, a re-test.

EXAMPLE:	I was sick the day the teacher gave the class the test. Luckily she's giving a **make-up**.
TRANSLATION:	I was sick the day the teacher gave the class the test. Luckily she's giving a **second chance to take it**.
"REAL SPEAK":	I w'z sick the day the teacher gave the class the test. Luckily she's giving a **make-up**.

NOW YOU DO IT:
(Use "make-up" in a sentence)

mid-term *n.* a test taken in the middle of the term which covers all the material learned up to that point.

EXAMPLE:	If I pass the biology **mid-term**, the rest of the course will be easy!
TRANSLATION:	If I pass the biology **test taken in the middle of the term**, the rest of the course will be easy!
"REAL SPEAK":	If I pass the bio **mid-term**, the rest 'a the course'll be easy!

NOW YOU DO IT:
(Use "mid-term" in a sentence)

pop quiz *n.* a surprise test (for which students aren't able to study in advance).

EXAMPLE:	My English teacher gave us a **pop quiz** today. Luckily I read all of the material last week!
TRANSLATION:	My English teacher gave us a **surprise test** today. Luckily I read all of the material last week!
"REAL SPEAK":	My English teacher gave us a **pop quiz** taday. Luckily I read all 'a the material last week!

NOW YOU DO IT:
(Use "pop quiz" in a sentence)

psych *n.* a common shortened name for "psychology."

EXAMPLE: I have to hurry. My **psych** class starts in five minutes and I don't want to be late!

TRANSLATION: I have to hurry. My **psychology** class starts in five minutes and I don't want to be late!

"REAL SPEAK": I hafta hurry. My **psych** class starts 'n five minutes 'n I don't wanna be late!

Note: Many other school courses have shortened names such as:

bio	=	biology
chem	=	chemistry
econ	=	economics
English lit	=	English literature
home ec	=	home economics
math	=	mathematics
P.E. or phys ed	=	physical education
poli sci	=	political science
"sosh"	=	sociology
trig	=	trigonometry

NOW YOU DO IT:

(Use "psych" in a sentence)

pull an all-nighter (to) *exp.* to stay up all night studying.

EXAMPLE: I'm exhausted. I **pulled an all-nighter** studying for my chemistry final.

TRANSLATION: I'm exhausted. I **stayed up all night** studying for my chemistry final.

"REAL SPEAK": I'm exhausted. I **pulled 'n all-nider** studying fer my chemistry final.

NOW YOU DO IT:

(Use "pull an all-nighter" in a sentence)

straight A's *exp.* perfect grades (in all subjects or all of one's exams).

EXAMPLE: Did you see Nancy's report card? She got **straight A's** for the third time!

TRANSLATION: Did you see Nancy's report card? She got **perfect grades** for the third time!

"REAL SPEAK": Did'ja see Nancy's report card? She got **straid A's** fer the third time!

NOW YOU DO IT:

(Use "straight A's" in a sentence)

LET'S PRACTICE!

A. TRUTH OR LIE *(Answers on p. 142)*

The students below are calling home. Read the conversation each student is having on the phone, then read their actual thoughts in the bubble. Decide if the student is telling the truth or a lie by checking the appropriate box.

READING
CD-B: TRACK 17

CD-B: TRACK 18

B. FIND THE DEFINITION *(Answers on p. 143)*

Write the definition of the slang word(s) in boldface choosing
from the word list below.

DEFINITIONS

to study very hard in a short period of time

to stay up all night studying

a common abbreviation for "psychology"

to miss class intentionally

extremely difficult or terrific

to do extremely poorly on a test

an end-of-term test which covers everything
learned during the school term

to remove a class from one's schedule

a test that can be taken again at a later time

perfect grades

a surprise test

to do extremely well on a test

1. **ace a test (to)** *exp.* to do extremely well on a test.

2. **blow a test (to)** *exp.* to do extremely poorly on a test

3. **cram (to)** *v.* to study hard in a short period of time

4. **cut class (to)** *exp.* to miss class intentionally

5. **drop a class (to)** *exp.* to remove a class from one's schedule

6. **final** *n.* end of term test.

7. **killer** *adj.* extremely difficult or terrific

8. **make-up / make-up test** *n.* a test can be taken again at a later time

9. **pop quiz** *n.* a surprise test

10. **psych** *n.* psychology

11. **pull an all-nighter (to)** *exp.* stay up all night studying

12. **straight A's** *exp.* perfect grades

C. FIND-THE-WORD GRID *(Answers on p. 143)*

Fill in the blanks with the most appropriate word using the list.
Next, find and circle the word in the grid below. Words may be
spelled vertically or horizontally.

CD-B: TRACK 19

aced	cut	flunk	pop	nighter
cram	drop	killer	psych	straight

1. I pulled an all- _nighter_ _____ studying for my history exam.

2. I _aced_ _____ my test! I got a perfect score!

3. My sister got the highest grade point average in our school. She got _straight_ _____ A's in every course!

4. I didn't see Ernie in school today. I wonder if he _cut_ _____ class again.

5. If you don't start to study harder, you're going to _blow_ _____ this course.

6. That was a _killer_ _____ test! I hope I pass!

7. I hate when the teacher gives us _pop_ _____ quizzes. I'd rather be able to prepare!

8. It's really ironic but I think our _psycho_ _____ teacher is crazy!

9. I'd like to go with you to the movies but I have to _cram_ _____ for a big test tomorrow morning.

10. This class is so hard! I think I might _drop_ _____ it and take something else.

FIND-THE-WORD GRID

T	N	W	U	F	S	A	C	E	D	G	R	R	E	W	D	W	T	M	A	T
H	O	H	T	O	E	G	R	O	A	O	O	E	D	H	S	E	O	E	M	A
V	W	Y	L	R	V	O	S	U	T	D	S	D	R	I	M	L	G	L	F	R
Y	T	S	T	R	A	I	G	H	T	I	E	A	O	C	E	L	O	U	L	V
E	H	O	W	K	N	U	R	T	N	P	S	N	P	O	P	I	H	N	U	E
I	I	T	O	O	Y	R	O	H	U	L	A	D	E	R	S	T	A	C	N	T
Q	I	T	X	R	E	F	U	C	N	E	R	V	B	E	Y	S	V	H	K	O
U	C	R	K	I	L	L	E	R	D	D	E	I	L	M	C	T	E	O	T	D
E	U	Y	W	N	R	T	H	A	E	G	R	N	I	G	H	T	E	R	O	E
I	T	T	W	D	S	H	T	M	R	E	E	L	E	N	N	M	O	I	S	A

LET'S REVIEW!

A FUN TIME WAS HAD BY ALL *(Answers on p. 143)*

Below are some slang terms and idioms you learned in previous lessons that are used to describe something fun to do in your free time. Write the number of the slang term or idiom from Column A next to its matching picture in Column B as well as next to the matching definition in Column C.

WRITING

COLUMN A	COLUMN B	COLUMN C
1. to grab a bite		4 to take a short drive
2. to take a dip	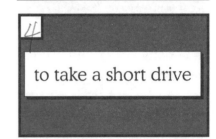	1 to go eat something
3. to hit the town		2 to go swimming
4. to take a spin		5 to go to the movies
5. to take in a movie		3 to go into town for dinner, movie, etc.

TO YOUR HEALTH

"I'm feeling under the weather!"

LET'S WARM UP!

MATCH THE PICTURES *(Answers on p. 144)*

As a fun way to get started, see if you can guess the meaning of the new slang words and expressions on the opposite page by using the pictures below and following the context of the sentences.

1. You're warm. Are you **running a fever**?
   - ☑ feverish
   - ☐ feeling energetic

2. It takes weeks to **bounce back** from the flu.
   - ☑ recover
   - ☐ to get sick again

3. Joan got dizzy and almost **passed out**.
   - ☐ woke up
   - ☑ fainted

4. I missed three weeks of work because I was **as sick as a dog**.
   - ☐ feeling great
   - ☑ feeling very sick

5. After being sick for a week, I'm finally back **in the pink**.
   - ☑ in good health
   - ☐ in poor health

6. There's nothing to do here. I'm **bored out of my mind**!
   - ☑ very bored
   - ☐ very excited

7. Don't work so hard. **Take it easy**!
   - ☑ relax
   - ☐ eat something

8. If I don't get out of this house, I'll **go stir crazy**!
   - ☐ go to sleep
   - ☑ become very restless from confinement

9. After a week of rest, you should be **raring to go**!
   - ☑ full of energy
   - ☐ exhausted

10. I can't sleep. I'm too **antsy**.
    - ☐ happy
    - ☑ nervous and agitated

11. Did your mother **pull through** after surgery?
    - ☐ get much worse
    - ☑ survive

12. You don't look well. Are you feeling **under the weather** today?
    - ☑ ill
    - ☐ healthy

13. There is no cure for a cold. You just have to let it **run its course**.
    - ☐ get better fast
    - ☑ lose strength on its own

14. I don't know what's wrong with me today. I don't really feel sick, just a little **blah**.
    - ☑ tired and lifeless
    - ☐ lively

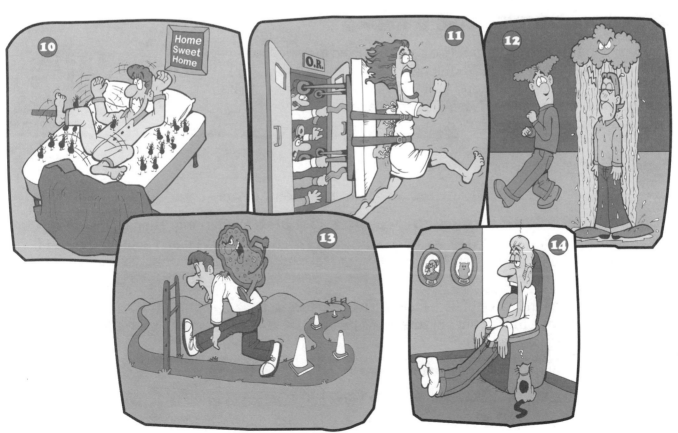

LET'S TALK!

A. DIALOGUE USING SLANG & IDIOMS

The words introduced on the first two pages are used in the following dialogue and illustrated in the long picture above. Can you understand the conversation and find the illustration that corresponds to the slang? *Note*: The translation of the words in boldface is on the right-hand page.

CD-B: TRACK 20

Karen and Janet are talking on the phone.

Karen: Hi, Janet. I haven't heard from you in a while. How are you?

Janet: I've been **feeling under the weather**. I felt **blah** all morning. Then by the afternoon, I was **as sick as a dog**. I started **running a fever** and actually thought I was going to **pass out**! Finally I had Brad take me to the doctor who said it was a bad case of the flu which just has to **run its course**. I should be **raring to go** soon.

Karen: Well, it sounds like you'll definitely **pull through**. It takes a while to **bounce back** after having the flu, but I'm sure you'll be back **in the pink** soon. Just try to **take it easy** for a while.

Janet: You're right, but I'm too **antsy** to just lie in bed. I get **bored out of my mind**.

Karen: I know what you mean. The last time I was sick, I started to **go stir crazy**!

B. DIALOGUE TRANSLATED INTO STANDARD ENGLISH

LET'S SEE HOW MUCH YOU REMEMBER!
Just for fun, bounce around in random order to the words and
expressions in boldface below. See if you can remember their slang
equivalents without looking at the left-hand page!

Karen and Janet are talking on the phone.

Karen: Hi, Janet. I haven't heard from you in a while. How are you?

Janet: I've been **feeling sick**. I felt **lifeless** all morning. Then by the afternoon, I was
extremely sick. I started **getting a fever** and actually thought I was going to
faint! Finally I had Brad take me to the doctor who said it was a bad case of the flu
which just has to **lose strength on its own**. I should be <u>**full of energy**</u> soon.

Karen: Well, it sounds like you'll definitely **survive**. It takes a while to **recover** after
having the flu, but I'm sure you'll be back **in good health** soon. Just try to <u>**relax**</u>
for a while.

Janet: You're right, but I'm too **restless** to just lie in bed. I get <u>**extremely bored**</u>.

Karen: I know what you mean. The last time I was sick, I started to **become very restless
<u>from being confined to one place</u>**!

C. DIALOGUE USING "REAL SPEAK"

The dialogue below demonstrates how the slang conversation on the previous page would *really* be spoken by native speakers!

CD-B: TRACK 20

Karen 'n Janet 'er talking on the phone.

Karen: Hi, Janet. I haven't heard fr'm ya in a while. How are ya?

Janet: I've been **feeling under the weather**. I felt **blah** all morning. Then by the afternoon, I w'z **ez sick ez a dog**. I starded **running a fever** 'n akshelly thod I w'z gonna **pass out**! Fin'lly I had Brad take me da the doctor who said it w'z a bad case 'a the flu which just hasta **run its course**. I should be **rarin' da go** soon.

Karen: Well, it sounds like you'll definitely **pull through**. It takes a while da **bounce back** after having the flu, bud I'm sher you'll be back **'n the pink** soon. Jus' try da **take id easy** fer a while.

Janet: Yer right bud I'm too **antsy** da jus' lie 'n bed. I get **bored oudda my mind**!

Karen: I know what'cha mean. The las' time I w'z sick, I starded ta **go stir crazy**!

KEY TO "REAL SPEAK"

YOU=YA • YOU'RE=Y'R • YOUR=YER • YOURS=YERS

The reduction of "you" to **ya** is so common, that you'll probably hear it within your first five minutes of being in the U.S.!

RULES

The "ou" sound in words like "you," "your," "you're," and "yours" typically involves puckering the lips. However in everyday speech, Americans tend to pronounce this so that there is no puckering of the lips at all, creating the reductions *ya, yer, y'r* and *yers*.

HOW DOES IT WORK?

STANDARD ENGLISH		"REAL SPEAK"
Do **you** feel under the weather? **You** look like you're running a fever.	you=ya ➡	Do **ya** feel under the weather? **Ya** look like you're running a fever.
Is that **your** sister? **Your** brother is going to pull through.	your=yer ➡	Is that **yer** sister? **Yer** brother is going to pull through.
You're my best friend. **You're** right!	you're=yer ➡	**Yer** my best friend. **Yer** right!
Is that computer **yours**? I love my PC, but **yours** is my favorite.	yours=yers ➡	Is that computer **yers**? I love my PC, but **yers** is my favorite.

BUT!

When "you" is stressed (indicated by the voice rising), it is <u>not</u> reduced to "**ya**":

–How are **ya**, Bill? –I'm fine, Ted. How are you?

LET'S USE "REAL SPEAK!"

A. UNSCRAMBLE *(Answers on p. 144)*

Step 1: Unscramble the word tiles and write the sentence below in box 1.

Step 2: Rewrite the sentence replacing **you**, **your**, **you're**, and **yours** with their real speak equivalents in box 2.

CD-B: TRACK 21

WHAT GET DID YOU YOUR BIRTHDAY FOR ?

1.
2.

GOING ARE YOU TO ? HOUSE MOTHER'S YOUR

1.
2.

YOU YOUR MONEY GAVE ALL YOUR BROTHER TO ?

1.
2.

YOU BEST KNOW MY YOU ARE . FRIEND

1.
2.

CAR WASHED TO GET TODAY YOU ARE GOING ? YOUR

1.
2.

LET'S LEARN!

VOCABULARY

The following words and expressions were used in the previous dialogues. Let's take a closer look at what they mean.

antsy (to be) *adj.* to be restless.

EXAMPLE: The movie was three hours long. After two hours, I started getting **antsy**.

TRANSLATION: The movie was three hours long. After two hours, I started getting **restless**.

"REAL SPEAK": The movie w'z three hours long. After two hours, I starded gedding **antsy**.

Synonym: **ants in one's pants (to have)** *exp.*

Note: Both expressions conjure up an image of ants crawling all over someone causing that person to squirm around and fidget.

NOW YOU DO IT:
(Create a sentence using "antsy")

blah (to feel) *adj.* to feel lifeless, generally a little tired and unfocused.

EXAMPLE: Thank you for inviting me to go with you, but I think I'm just going to stay home tonight. I'm feeling a little **blah**.

TRANSLATION: Thank you for inviting me to go with you, but I think I'm just going to stay home tonight. I'm feeling a little **tired and unfocused**.

"REAL SPEAK": Thanks fer inviding me da go with you, b'd I think I'm jus' gonna stay home tanight. I'm feeling a liddle **blah**.

Synonym 1: **out of it (to feel)** *exp.*
Synonym 2: **out of sorts (to feel)** *exp.*
Synonym 3: **to be oneself (not)** *exp.*

NOW YOU DO IT:
(Create a sentence using "blah")

bored out of one's mind (to be) *exp.* to be very bored.

EXAMPLE: I was **bored out of my mind** during the lecture! I couldn't wait for it to end!

TRANSLATION: I was **terribly bored** during the lecture! I couldn't wait for it to end!

"REAL SPEAK": I w'z **bored oudda my min'** during the lecture! I couldn' wait for it ta end!

Synonym 1: **bored out of one's skull (to be)** *exp.*
Synonym 2: **bored stiff (to be)** *exp.*

NOW YOU DO IT:
(Create a sentence using "bored out of one's mind")

bounce back (to) *v.* to recover.

EXAMPLE: Dan is taking a long time to **bounce back** from the flu. He must be really sick.

TRANSLATION: Dan is taking a long time to **recover** from the flu. He must be really sick.

"REAL SPEAK": Dan's taking a long time da **bounce back** fr'm the flu. He mus' be really sick.

NOW YOU DO IT:

(Create a sentence using "bounce back")

in the pink (to be) *exp.* to be enjoying good health (exhibited by a healthy pink color of one's skin).

EXAMPLE: My father is feeling much better. He's finally **in the pink** again.

TRANSLATION: My father is feeling much better. He's finally **enjoying good health** again.

"REAL SPEAK": My dad's feeling much bedder. He's fin'lly **in the pink** again.

NOW YOU DO IT:

(Create a sentence using "in the pink")

pass out (to) *v.* to faint.

EXAMPLE: Jody **passed out** after working out at the gym. I think he exercised too hard!

TRANSLATION: Jody **fainted** after working out at the gym. I think he exercised too hard!

"REAL SPEAK": Jody **passed oud** after working oud at the gym. I think 'e exercised too hard!

NOW YOU DO IT:

(Create a sentence using "pass out")

pull through (to) *v.* to survive.

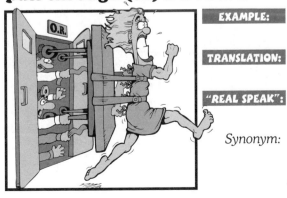

EXAMPLE: Don't worry. I'm sure Debbie will **pull through**. The doctors say she's getting better every day.

TRANSLATION: Don't worry. I'm sure Debbie will **survive**. The doctors say she's getting better every day.

"REAL SPEAK": Don't worry. I'm sher Debbie'll **pull through**. The docters say she's gedding bedder ev'ry day.

Synonym: **make it (to)** *exp.*

NOW YOU DO IT:

(Create a sentence using "pull through")

raring to go (to be) *exp.* to be energetic (and ready to seize the moment).

> **EXAMPLE:** I know you feel blah right now but after a good night's sleep, I'm sure you'll be **raring to go**!
>
> **TRANSLATION:** I know you feel blah right now but after a good night's sleep, I'm sure you'll be **energetic**!
>
> **"REAL SPEAK":** I know ya feel blah right now bud after a good night's sleep, I'm sher you'll be **rarin' da go**!
>
> *Synonym:* **up and at them (to be)** *exp.*
>
> *Note:* This expression is always reduced to: **to be up 'n ad 'em.**
>
> **NOW YOU DO IT:**
>
> *(Create a sentence using "raring to go")*

run a fever (to) *exp.* to have a high body temperature, to be feverish.

> **EXAMPLE:** If you start to **run a fever**, you should go see your doctor right away.
>
> **TRANSLATION:** If you start to **get a high body temperature**, you should go see your doctor right away.
>
> **"REAL SPEAK":** If ya start ta **run a fever**, you should go see yer docter ride away.
>
> **NOW YOU DO IT:**
>
> *(Create a sentence using "run a fever")*

run its course (to) *exp.* said of an illness that will lose strength on its own over time.

> **EXAMPLE:** Unfortunately, there's no treatment for the common cold yet. It just has to **run its course**.
>
> **TRANSLATION:** Unfortunately, there's no treatment for the common cold yet. It just has to **lose strength on its own over time**.
>
> **"REAL SPEAK":** Unfortunately, there's no treatment fer the common cold yet. It just hasta **run its course**.
>
> **NOW YOU DO IT:**
>
> *(Create a sentence using "run its course")*

sick as a dog (to be as) *exp.* to be extremely sick.

> **EXAMPLE:** Usually I never get sick. But last week I was **as sick as a dog**! Luckily, I'm doing a lot better now.
>
> **TRANSLATION:** Usually I never get sick. But last week I was **extremely sick**! Luckily, I'm doing a lot better now.
>
> **"REAL SPEAK":** Usually I never get sick. B't last week I w'z **'ez sick 'ez a dog**! Luckily, I'm doing a lot bedder now.
>
> **NOW YOU DO IT:**
>
> *(Create a sentence using "sick as a dog")*

stir crazy (to go) *exp.* to become very restless from being confined to one place.

EXAMPLE: I wish it would stop raining so I could go outside. I've been locked up in this house for almost a week and I'm starting to **go stir crazy**!

TRANSLATION: I wish it would stop raining so we could go outside. I've been locked up in this house for almost a week and I'm starting to **become very restless from being confined to one place**!

"REAL SPEAK": I wish it'd stop raining so we could go outside. I've been locked up 'n this house fer almost a week 'n I'm starding ta **go stir crazy**!

NOW YOU DO IT:

(Create a sentence using "stir crazy")

take it easy (to) *exp.* to relax.

EXAMPLE: Ralph works so hard all the time. I'm worried that if he doesn't start to slow down and **take it easy**, he's going to get sick!

TRANSLATION: Ralph works so hard all the time. I'm worried that if he doesn't start to slow down and **relax**, he's going to get sick!

"REAL SPEAK": Ralph works so hard all the time. I'm worried thad if 'e doesn't start ta slow down 'n **take id easy**, he's gonna get sick!

NOW YOU DO IT:

(Create a sentence using "take it easy")

under the weather (to feel) *exp.* to feel sick.

EXAMPLE: Hi, Richard. You look a little tired today. Have you been **feeling under the weather**?

TRANSLATION: Hi, Richard. You look a little tired today. Have you been **feeling sick**?

"REAL SPEAK": Hi, Richard. You look a liddle tired taday. Have you been **feeling under the weather**?

NOW YOU DO IT:

(Create a sentence using "feel under the weather")

LET'S PRACTICE!

A. THE UNFINISHED CONVERSATION *(Answers on p. 144)*

Read the conversations then fill in the last line with your own words in response to what you've just read. Make sure to use the suggested words in your response. Your response can be in the form of a question or statement.

CD-B: TRACK 23

1

Jodi: Would you like to go to the movies tonight?

Angela: I'd like to but I've been **feeling a little under the weather**. Maybe I'd better just stay home.

Jodi: _____

use: **stir crazy**

2

Steve: Where have you been? I haven't seen you at school.

Al: I was **as sick as a dog**. I was **running a high fever** all week!

Steve: _____

use: **run its course**

3

Kim: I can't stand biology class. I don't know how I'm going to be able to dissect frogs today. I hope I don't get dizzy and **pass out**!

Doug: Just **take it easy**. You'll **pull through** just fine.

Kim: _____

use: **as sick as a dog**

4

Nick: The doctor said you have to **take it easy** until the flu **runs its course**.

Tessa: But I'm so **antsy** being inside all day! I'm **bored out of my mind**!

Nick: _____

use: **in the pink**

5

Carl: Good to see you again. Have you **bounced back** from that virus?

Sandy: Yeah, I'm feeling much better. I was **going stir crazy** lying in bed all day long. I hope you didn't catch it.

Carl: _____

use: **feel blah**

CD-B: TRACK 24

B. CHOOSE THE RIGHT WORD *(Answers on p. 144)*

Underline the appropriate word that best completes the phrase.

1. I'm feeling a little (**under**, **over**, **behind**) the weather today. I hope I'm not catching a cold. I have to go to work tonight!

2. I haven't gone outside for three days because I've been sick. I'm starting to go stir (**happy**, **hungry**, **crazy**)!

3. I've been cold all day and it's the middle of summer! I wonder if I'm (**skipping**, **walking**, **running**) a fever.

4. My mother caught the flu last week and was sick as a (**cat**, **giraffe**, **dog**).

5. You really don't need to worry at all. The surgeon said Monica will (**pull**, **push**, **lift**) through just fine.

6. Let's go to the movies. I want to do something fun. I've been bored out of my (**brain**, **mind**, **eyes**) all day!

7. Unfortunately, there's no cure for a virus. You just have to let it (**run**, **jog**, **walk**) its course.

8. I was sick for two weeks but I'm finally in the (**green**, **yellow**, **pink**)!

9. I don't feel sick or anything. I just feel kind of (**blue**, **blond**, **blah**).

10. You've been sick for a long time, so don't exercise too hard yet. It takes a while to bounce (**back**, **around**, **up**) after having the flu.

11. I feel like I'm going to pass (**up**, **in**, **out**). I need to sit down.

12. Why are you (**antsy**, **fancy**, **in the pink**) today? You need to calm down!

13. You're working too hard. You really need to take it (**hard**, **easy**, **simple**).

14. After a few days of rest, you'll be raring to (**go**, **stop**, **move**).

C. COMPLETE THE STORY *(Answers on p. 145)*
Use the illustrations to help you fill in the blanks with the
correct slang term or expression.

CD-B: TRACK 25

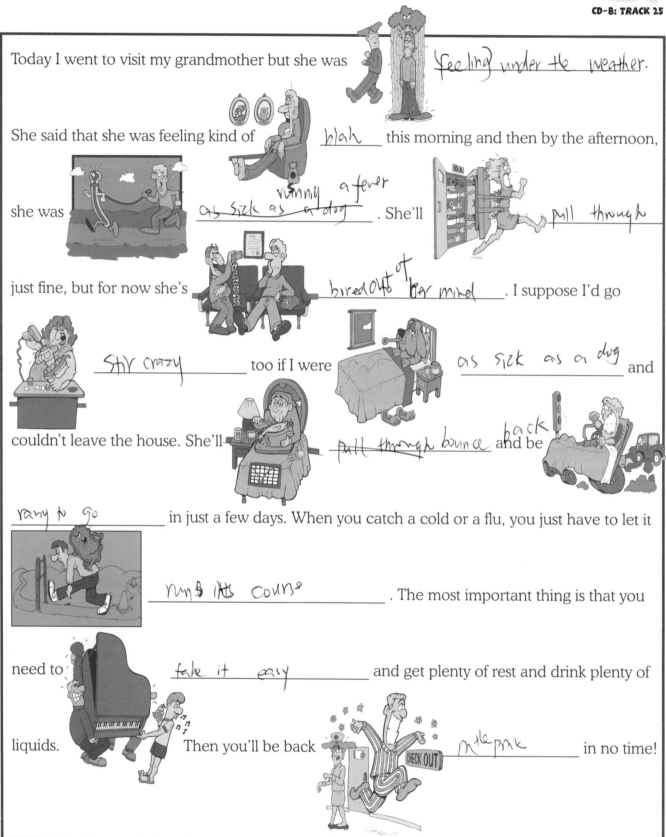

Today I went to visit my grandmother but she was _feeling under the weather._

She said that she was feeling kind of _blah_ this morning and then by the afternoon,

she was _as sick as a dog_ _runny a fever_. She'll _pull through_

just fine, but for now she's _bored out of her mind_. I suppose I'd go

stir crazy too if I were _as sick as a dog_ and

couldn't leave the house. She'll ~~pull through~~ _bounce back_ and be

rary to go in just a few days. When you catch a cold or a flu, you just have to let it

run its course. The most important thing is that you

need to _take it easy_ and get plenty of rest and drink plenty of

liquids. Then you'll be back _in the pink_ in no time!

LET'S REVIEW!

THE NIGHT SHIFT *(Answers on p. 146)*

In previous lessons, you have learned some slang terms and idioms used to describe something that happens at night. Write the number of the slang term or idiom from Column A next to its matching picture in Column B as well as next to the matching definition in Column C.

COLUMN A	COLUMN B	COLUMN C
1. to pull an all-nighter		**5** to lodge
2. rush hour		**2** the time when most drivers are on the road
3. to stay up till all hours of the night		**3** to stay up all night
4. red-eye		**4** overnight flight
5. to put up for the night		**1/2** to stay up all night studying

"He stood me up!"

LET'S WARM UP!

MATCH THE PICTURES *(Answers on p. 146)*

As a fun way to get started, see if you can guess the meaning of the new slang words and expressions on the opposite page by using the pictures below and following the context of the sentences.

1. They're not old enough to know true love. It's just **puppy love**.
   Definition: "immature love"
   ☑ True ☐ False

2. Cathy's smiling at you. Maybe she has a **crush on** you!
   Definition: "dislike for"
   ☐ True ☑ False

3. That's your wife? When did you **tie the knot**?
   Definition: "get married"
   ☑ True ☐ False

4. There are **no strings attached** to my invitation. I don't expect anything in return.
   Definition: "hidden motives"
   ☑ True ☐ False

5. If you don't want to go out with Bill, **turn him down**.
   Definition: "decline his offer"
   ☑ True ☐ False

6. John is definitely not a hunk. He's the biggest **nerd**!
   Definition: "athlete"
   ☐ True ☑ False

7. My boyfriend **dumped** me for another girl!
   Definition: "rejected"
   ☑ True ☐ False

8. Ted was late, but he finally **showed up**.
   Definition: "appeared"
   ☑ True ☐ False

9. I waited an hour for him. He **stood me up**!
   Definition: "finally arrived"
   ☐ True ☑ False

10. When I met your father, it was **love at first sight**.
    Definition: "instant love"
    ☑ True ☐ False

11. Tessa is **drop-dead gorgeous**! Is she a model?
    Definition: "very beautiful"
    ☑ True ☐ False

12. Leonard and I planned on having dinner together last night, but he had **to break our date**.
    Definition: "to cancel our date"
    ☑ True ☐ False

13. If you don't really like Martin, don't go out with him. You're just **leading him on**!
    Definition: "making him falsely think you're interested in him"
    ☑ True ☐ False

14. If you want a date with Jennifer, just **ask her out**!
    Definition: "ask her on a date"
    ☑ True ☐ False

15. I heard you went out on a **blind date** last night! Did you know what he looked like before you met him?
    Definition: "date with someone you know well"
    ☐ True ☑ False

LET'S TALK!

A. DIALOGUE USING SLANG & IDIOMS

The words introduced on the first two pages are used in the following dialogue and illustrated in the long picture above. Can you understand the conversation and find the illustration that corresponds to the slang? *Note*: The translation of the words in boldface is on the right-hand page.

CD-B: TRACK 26

Susan is telling Melanie about her date.

Melanie: You have to tell me about your **blind date**. How was it? Was he **drop-dead gorgeous**? Was it **love at first sight**?

Susan: Hardly! First of all, I waited for an hour before he finally picked me up. I just assumed that he **stood me up**. Then when he finally did **show up**, I opened the door to find the biggest **nerd** standing there! By the end of the evening, he told me that he had a **crush on** me and then started talking about **tying the knot**!

Melanie: On the first date?! It was probably just **puppy love**. Listen, my advice to you is that the next time he **asks you out**, just **turn him down** and run in the opposite direction! Whatever you do, you certainly don't want to **lead him on**.

Susan: I'm supposed to go out with another guy next week, but I've decided to **break our date**. I just can't go through this again.

M̶̶̶̶ ̶̶w, don't **dump** him before you even meet him! He may be a great guy for you. Just ̶̶e sure there are **no strings attached** before you go out.

 You go out with him.

B. DIALOGUE TRANSLATED INTO STANDARD ENGLISH

LET'S SEE HOW MUCH YOU REMEMBER!
Just for fun, bounce around in random order to the words and expressions in boldface below. See if you can remember their slang equivalents without looking at the left-hand page!

Susan is telling Melanie about her date.

Melanie: You have to tell me about your **date with the person you've never met before**. How was it? Was he **extremely attractive**? Was it **immediate love upon seeing him for the first time**?

Susan: Hardly! First of all, I waited for an hour before he finally picked me up. I just assumed that he **intentionally didn't arrive for our date**. Then when he finally did **arrive**, I opened the door to find the biggest **social misfit** standing there! By the end of the evening, he told m that he had an **infatuation with** me and then started talking about **getting married**!

Melanie: On the first date?! It was probably just **immature love between young people**. Listen, my advice to you is that the next time he **invites you to go on a date**, just **decline** and run in the opposite direction! Whatever you do, you certainly don't want to **make him falsely think that you're interested in him**.

Susan: I'm supposed to go out with another guy next week, but I've decided to **cancel the date**. I just can't go through this again.

Melanie: Now, don't **end the relationship** with him before you even meet him! He may be a great guy for you. Just make sure there are **no hidden motives** before you go out.

Susan: Fine. _You_ go out with him.

C. DIALOGUE USING "REAL SPEAK"

The dialogue below demonstrates how the slang conversation on the previous page would *really* be spoken by native speakers!

CD-B: TRACK 26

Susan's telling Melanie aboud 'er date.

Melanie: Ya hafta tell me about cher **blin' date**. How was it? Was 'e **drop-dead gorgeous**? Was it **love 'it firs' sight**?

Susan: Hardly! First of all, I waided fer 'n hour b'fore 'e fin'lly picked me up. I just assumed th'd I w'z being **stood up**. Then when 'e fin'lly did **show up**, I open' the door da fin' the bigges' **nerd** standing there! By the end 'a the ev'ning, he told me thad 'e had a **crush on** me an' then starded talking about **tying the knot**!

Melanie: On the firs' date?! It w'z prob'ly jus' **puppy love**. Listen, my advice ta you is that the nex' time 'e **asks you out**, jus' **turn 'im down** an' run 'n the opposite direction! Whadever ya do, ya certainly don't wanna **lead 'im on**.

Susan: I'm sapposta go out with another guy next week, b'd I've decided ta **break 'ar date**. I jus' can't go through this again.

Melanie: Now, don't **dump** 'im b'fore ya even meed 'im! He may be a great guy fer you. Jus' make sher there'er **no strings attached** b'fore ya go out.

Susan: Fine. *You* go out with 'im.

KEY TO "REAL SPEAK"

HAVE TO = HAFTA • HAS TO = HASTA

In the above dialogue using "real speak," "have to" became **hafta**. This is an extremely common reduction used by everyone!

RULES

Rule 1: When "have" is followed by "to," the combination is commonly pronounced **hafta**.
Rule 2: When "has" is followed by "to," the combination is commonly pronouced **hasta**.

HOW DOES IT WORK?

I **have to break our date.**

I ha**v**~~e~~ to break our date.
↓
I ha**f** to break our date.

} In the phrase "have to," the "e" is silent and the "v" sound changes to "f."

I haf t**o** break our date.
↓
I haf t**uh** break our date.

} Many unstressed vowels (such as the **o** in "to") are commonly pronounced **uh**.

⬇   ⬇

I **hafta** break our date.

This reduced version of "have to" is so common in everyday speech that it is often seen written in magazines and newspapers when quoting spoken language.

THE HAFTA / HASTA CHART

	SINGULAR		PLURAL				SINGULAR		PLURAL	
1st person	I	*have to*	We	*have to*		1st person	I	**hafta**	We	**hafta**
2nd person	You	*have to*	You	*have to*		2nd person	You	**hafta**	You	**hafta**
3rd person	He She It }	*has to*	They	*have to*		3rd person	He She It }	**hasta**	They	**hafta**

LET'S USE "REAL SPEAK!"

A. NOW YOU HAFTA DO A "HAFTA" EXERCISE *(Answers on p. 147)*

Fill in each box deciding when to use "hafta" and when to use "hasta." Most important, practice speaking the paragraph in real speak using your answers.

CD-B: TRACK 27

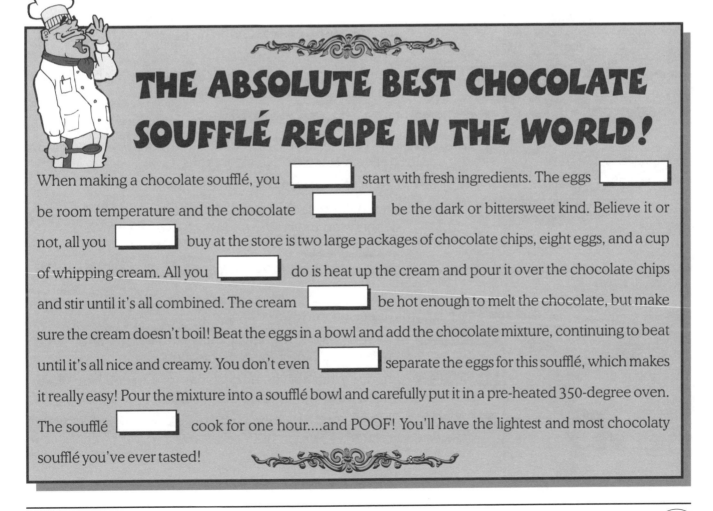

THE ABSOLUTE BEST CHOCOLATE SOUFFLÉ RECIPE IN THE WORLD!

When making a chocolate soufflé, you [ ] start with fresh ingredients. The eggs [ ] be room temperature and the chocolate [ ] be the dark or bittersweet kind. Believe it or not, all you [ ] buy at the store is two large packages of chocolate chips, eight eggs, and a cup of whipping cream. All you [ ] do is heat up the cream and pour it over the chocolate chips and stir until it's all combined. The cream [ ] be hot enough to melt the chocolate, but make sure the cream doesn't boil! Beat the eggs in a bowl and add the chocolate mixture, continuing to beat until it's all nice and creamy. You don't even [ ] separate the eggs for this soufflé, which makes it really easy! Pour the mixture into a soufflé bowl and carefully put it in a pre-heated 350-degree oven. The soufflé [ ] cook for one hour....and POOF! You'll have the lightest and most chocolaty soufflé you've ever tasted!

LET'S LEARN!

CD-B: TRACK 28

VOCABULARY

The following words and expressions were used in the previous dialogues. Let's take a closer look at what they mean.

ask someone out (to) *exp.* to invite someone to go on a date.

EXAMPLE:	Don't be so scared. Just **ask her out**. The worst thing she could say is no.
TRANSLATION:	Don't be so scared. Just **invite her to go on a date with you**. The worst thing she could say is no.
"REAL SPEAK":	Don't be so scared. Just **ask 'er out**. The wors' thing she could say is no.

NOW YOU DO IT:

(Create a sentence using "ask someone out")

blind date *n.* • **1.** a date with someone you have never met in person • **2.** a person you are going on a date with that you have never seen in person.

EXAMPLE 1:	Tonight I'm going on a **blind date**. I hope he's better than the last one. He was so horrible!
TRANSLATION:	Tonight I'm going on a **date with someone I've never met before**. I hope he's better than the last one. He was so horrible!
"REAL SPEAK":	Tanight I'm going on a **blin' date**. I hope 'e's bedder th'n the last one. He w'z so horrible!
EXAMPLE 2:	Did you see Tina's **blind date**? He's gorgeous!
TRANSLATION:	Did you see Tina's **date that she's never seen in person before**? He's gorgeous!
"REAL SPEAK":	Did'ja see **Tina's blin'** date? He's gorgeous!
Note:	The difference between definitions **1.** and **2.** simply depends on the context.

NOW YOU DO IT:

(Create a sentence using "blind date")

break a date (to) *exp.* to cancel a date.

EXAMPLE:	I'm sorry but I'm going to have to **break our date**. I need to go out of town on business.
TRANSLATION:	I'm sorry but I'm going to have to **cancel our date**. I need to go out of town on business.
"REAL SPEAK":	I'm sorry bud I'm gonna hafta **break 'ar date**. I need ta go oudda town on business.

NOW YOU DO IT:

(Create a sentence using "break a date")

crush on someone (to have a) *exp.* to have an infatuation with someone.

EXAMPLE: I think Betty has a **crush on** me. She keeps following me everywhere!

TRANSLATION: I think Betty has an **infatuation with** me. She keeps following me everywhere!

"REAL SPEAK": I think Betty has a **crush on** me. She keeps following me ev'rywhere!

NOW YOU DO IT:

(Create a sentence using "have a crush on someone")

drop-dead gorgeous *exp.* extremely beautiful.

EXAMPLE: Nancy's children are **drop-dead gorgeous**! It wouldn't surprise me if they became movie stars.

TRANSLATION: Nancy's children are **extremely beautiful**! It wouldn't surprise me if they became movie stars.

"REAL SPEAK": Nancy's children 'er **drop-dead gorgeous**! It wouldn't saprise me if they b'came movie stars.

Synonym: **babe (to be a)** *n.*

NOW YOU DO IT:

(Create a sentence using "drop-dead gorgeous")

dump someone (to) *v.* to end a relationship with someone.

EXAMPLE: My boyfriend just **dumped me** because he saw me with another man and that man was my brother!

TRANSLATION: My boyfriend just **ended our relationship** because he saw me with another man and that man was my brother!

"REAL SPEAK": My boyfrien' just **dumped me** cuz 'e saw me with another man an' that man w'z my brother!

NOW YOU DO IT:

(Create a sentence using "dump someone")

lead someone on (to) *exp.* to make someone falsely think that there is mutual interest.

EXAMPLE: You have to be honest and stop **leading him on**. Just tell him that you're not interested in him.

TRANSLATION: You have to be honest and stop **making him think you like him when you don't**. Just tell him that you're not interested in him.

"REAL SPEAK": Ya hafta be honest 'n stop **leading 'im on**. Jus' tell 'im that ch'r nod int'rested in 'im.

NOW YOU DO IT:

(Create a sentence using "lead someone on")

love at first sight *exp.* instant love upon seeing someone for the first time.

EXAMPLE: When I met your father twenty years ago, it was **love at first sight**.

TRANSLATION: When I met your father twenty years ago, it was **instant love upon seeing him**.

"REAL SPEAK": When I met ch'r father twen'y years ago, it w'z **love 'it firs' sight**.

NOW YOU DO IT:

(Create a sentence using "love at first sight")

nerd *n.* a social misfit, someone who is out-of-date in appearance and unsophisticated.

EXAMPLE: I've never met anyone who is so boring! And you should have seen the way he dresses. What a **nerd**!

TRANSLATION: I've never met anyone who is so boring! And you should have seen the way he dresses. What a **social misfit**!

"REAL SPEAK": I've never med anyone who's so boring! An' you should'ev seen the way he dresses. Whad a **nerd**!

NOW YOU DO IT:

(Create a sentence using "nerd")

no strings attached *exp.* with no hidden expectations, no hidden motives.

EXAMPLE: Would you like to go to the movies tonight? **No strings attached**.

TRANSLATION: Would you like to go to the movies tonight? **No hidden motives**.

"REAL SPEAK": Would'ja like ta go da the movies tanight? **No strings attached**.

NOW YOU DO IT:

(Create a sentence using "no strings attached")

puppy love *exp.* immature love between young people or children.

EXAMPLE: I think my little son likes your little daughter. **Puppy love** is so sweet!

TRANSLATION: I think my little son likes your little daughter. **Immature love between young children** is so sweet!

"REAL SPEAK": I think my liddle son likes yer liddle daughter. **Puppy love** is so sweet!

NOW YOU DO IT:

(Create a sentence using "puppy love")

show up (to) *exp.* to arrive.

EXAMPLE: You won't believe what time Noah finally **showed up**... two o'clock in the morning!

TRANSLATION: You won't believe what time Noah finally **arrived**... two o'clock in the morning!

"REAL SPEAK": You won't b'lieve what time Noah fin'lly **showed up**... two a'clock 'n the morning!

NOW YOU DO IT:
(Create a sentence using "show up")

stand someone up (to) *exp.* to fail to arrive for a date.

EXAMPLE: Greg was supposed to meet me at seven o'clock for dinner, but he never arrived! This is the last time he's going to **stand me up**!

TRANSLATION: Greg was supposed to meet me at seven o'clock for dinner, but he never arrived! This is the last time he's going to **fail to arrive for a date with me**!

"REAL SPEAK": Greg w'z sapposta meet me 'it seven a'clock fer dinner, bud 'e never arrived! This is the las' time 'e's gonna **stan' me up**!

NOW YOU DO IT:
(Create a sentence using "stand someone up")

tie the knot (to) *exp.* to get married.

EXAMPLE: I heard you and Nicholas **tied the knot** last month! Congratulations!

TRANSLATION: I heard you and Nicholas **got married** last month! Congratulations!

"REAL SPEAK": I heard'ju 'n Nicholas **tied the knot** las' month! C'ngradjalations!

NOW YOU DO IT:
(Create a sentence using "tie the knot")

turn someone down (to) *exp.* to decline someone's offer of going on a date.

EXAMPLE: I never should have listened to you. When I asked Sally out, she **turned me down**!

TRANSLATION: I never should have listened to you. When I asked Sally out, she **declined my offer**!

"REAL SPEAK": I never should'a listen' da you. When I asked Sally out, she **turn' me down**!

NOW YOU DO IT:
(Create a sentence using "turn someone down")

LET'S PRACTICE!

A. CREATE YOUR OWN STORY - *(Part 1) (Answers on p. 147)*

Follow the instructions below and write down your answer in the space provided. When you have finished answering all the questions, transfer your answers to the story on the opposite page. Make sure to match the number of your answer with the numbered space in the story.

1. Write down a "thing" *(pencil, potato, toothbrush, etc.)*:

    _____

2. Write down a "man's name":

    _____

3. Write down a "body part":

    _____

4. Write down an "adjective" *(big, small, pretty, etc.)*:

    _____

5. Write down "something you eat":

    _____

6. Write down "any kind of liquid":

    _____

7. Write down another "kind of liquid":

    _____

8. Write down a "thing":

    _____

9. Write down another "thing":

    _____

10. Write down a "body part":

    _____

11. Write down a "mode of transportation":

    _____

12. Write down a "thing":

    _____

13. Write down another "thing":

    _____

14. Write down another "thing":

    _____

B. CREATE YOUR OWN STORY - *(Part 2)*

Once you've filled in the blanks, read your story aloud. If you've done Part 1 correctly, you're story should be hilarious!

SPEAKING

THE WEEKLY
Cupid Gazette

THE WEEKLY NEWSPAPER THAT PROVES LOVE IS ALWAYS IN THE AIR

"Dear Gabby..."

by Gabby Blabber
Advice Columnist

Dear Gabby...

Today, I went out on a blind date with a _____ [1.] named _____ [2.]. At first I thought I was being stood up because he showed up late. But when I took one look at his _____ [3.], it was

love at first sight! He took me to a _____ [4.] restaurant that serves large portions of _____ [5.] covered in _____ [6.]. We even drank an expensive bottle of _____ [7.] with dinner. Everything was going great until a drop-dead gorgeous _____ [8.] suddenly walked into the room wearing an extremely tiny _____ [9.]. He just couldn't take his _____ [10.] off her. I'm sure he had a crush on her

that was more than just puppy love. I was so mad that I dumped him right there and went home by _____ [11.]. Yesterday, he called me on the _____ [12.] and apologized for being such a _____ [13.]. In fact, he even asked me out again. When I turned him down, he kept begging me to give him one more _____ [14.]. What should I do?

signed... *Confused*

C. **WHAT WOULD YOU DO IF SOMEONE SAID...?** (Answers on p. 147)

What would you do in response to the words in white italics?
Choose your answer by placing an "X" in the box.

CD-B: TRACK 29

1.	*Oh, darling! I love you so much. Let's tie the knot!*	I would... ☐ a. bend down and tie my shoe ☐ b. make wedding plans ☐ c. get some rope
2.	*I've been waiting here for an hour. I was beginning to think you stood me up!*	I would... ☐ a. offer an apology ☐ b. offer to hold them upright for an hour ☐ c. offer to fix their car
3.	*I can't hide my feelings any longer. I have a crush on you.*	I would... ☐ a. crush that person back ☐ b. put that person in a headlock ☐ c. tell the person your true feelings
4.	*My aunt is in the hospital. I'm afraid I'm going to have to break our date.*	I would... ☐ a. get a broom to clean up the mess ☐ b. try to make plans for a later time ☐ c. offer to help break it
5.	*Where did you get those clothes? You dress like such a nerd!*	I would... ☐ a. thank the person for the compliment ☐ b. run out and buy new clothing ☐ c. buy more clothing in the same style
6.	*There's Karen. She's drop-dead gorgeous!*	I would... ☐ a. quickly try to revive her ☐ b. call an ambulance ☐ c. agree and explain that she's a model
7.	*My girlfriend just dumped me. What should I do?*	I would... ☐ a. offer to pick him back up ☐ b. offer to get him a bandage ☐ c. offer advice
8.	*I think you're very nice. I'd like to ask you out for Saturday night.*	I would... ☐ a. accept and suggest going to a movie ☐ b. accept but insist on staying indoors ☐ c. accept and go stand outside
9.	*Thank you for inviting me to the party but I have to turn you down.*	I would... ☐ a. tell him that I'll see him there ☐ b. tell him that I'm disappointed ☐ c. tell him to take the elevator instead
10.	*Let's go out tonight and just have fun. No strings attached.*	I would... ☐ a. suggest that chains really are stronger ☐ b. agree to go ☐ c. argue that violins are better than horns

LET'S REVIEW!

SOME OPPOSITES DO ATTRACT! *(Answers on p. 147)*

Now that you've learned almost 200 slang terms and idioms, this review exercise should be a piece of cake (which means "easy" in slang)! Match the picture in Column A with the picture in Column B that has the opposite meaning by connecting the dots next to each picture.

COLUMN A	COLUMN B
1. hunk	**A.** to blow a test
2. to be unable to stand someone	**B.** to dump someone
3. to tie the knot	**C.** to be in the pink
4. to feel under the weather	**D.** nerd
5. to ace a test	**E.** to have a crush on someone

ANSWERS TO LESSONS 1-10

LESSON ONE – AT THE PARTY

LET'S WARM UP!

1. Get control of your emotions
2. having a great time
3. What's wrong with him?
4. I think it's a hairpiece
5. You're kidding me

6. Look at that dress
7. He's a muscular man
8. That's impossible!
9. Stop nagging me!
10. I can't tolerate her

LET'S USE "REAL SPEAK"

A. WHA'DID THEY SAY?

1. b
2. a
3. a

4. a
5. a
6. a

LET'S PRACTICE!

A. CONTEXT EXERCISE

1. makes sense
2. makes sense
3. doesn't make sense
4. doesn't make sense
5. makes sense

6. makes sense
7. doesn't make sense
8. makes sense
9. doesn't make sense

B. CHOOSE THE RIGHT WORD

1. upset
2. muscular
3. on
4. blast
5. up

6. of
7. hair
8. mean
9. case
10. No

C. COMPLETE THE PHRASE

1. what's up
2. get a grip
3. putting me on
4. on my case
5. blast

6. can't stand
7. no way
8. rug
9. hunk

D. IS IT "YES" OR IS IT "NO?" (POSSIBLE ANSWERS)

1. Yes. He's a hunk.
2. No. I can't stand her.
3. No. I'm putting you on.
4. No. I think it's a rug.
5. Yes. He needs to get a grip.

6. Yes. She got on my case.
7. Yes. I got a load of it.
8. No. No way!
9. Yes. I had a blast!
10. Yes. What's up with his eye?

LESSON TWO – AT THE MARKET
LET'S WARM UP!

1. C
2. A
3. E
4. G
5. F

6. J
7. I
8. D
9. H
10. B

LET'S USE "REAL SPEAK"

A. "T" PRONOUNCED LIKE "D"

1. Wha**t** a beau**t**iful swea**t**er! Did you ge**t** it when you went shopping last Sa**t**urday?

2. My parents ordered a bo**tt**le of champagne for their anniversary.

3. My laptop compu**t**er is ba**tt**ery-opera**t**ed.

4. Wha**t** a great car! Is i**t** an au**t**oma**t**ic?

5. Let's go **t**o the par**t**y la**t**er. Be**tt**y said there's going to be a lo**t** of good food there.

6. What ci**t**y do you live in?

7. Would you like a soft drink or a bo**tt**le of wa**t**er?

8. Did you invi**t**e that pre**tt**y girl to your house for a li**tt**le dinner?

9. I just bough**t** a po**tt**ed plant. It's a beau**t**iful bonsai tree.

10. Wha**t** a pi**t**y about your li**tt**le sister's babysi**tt**er. I heard she go**t** into a car accident!

LET'S PRACTICE!

A. TV COMMERCIAL

1. In the produce department, they have veggies.
2. You won't have to wait in line because there are ten checkers waiting to ring up your order.
3. The announcer suggests that you pick up lemon cake from the bakery.
4. They are lowering prices of vegetables at David's Market.
5. The lemon sponge cake is to die for!
6. Yes, the market has everything I need to make a wonderful dessert from scratch.

B. YOU'RE THE AUTHOR

Joe: We need to **pick up** some **veggies** like lettuce, cucumber, and tomatoes for our salad tonight. And you're going to love this store. They've **slashed** their prices on everything this week.

Kim: You're right! I've never seen such **rock**-bottom prices. At my store, everything is so expensive. Yesterday I paid five dollars for bread! What a **rip-off**!

Joe: You're not kidding! Hey, I have an idea. Instead of buying dessert, let's make one from **scratch**...something with chocolate. I have a recipe that's **to die for**!

Kim: You're making my **mouth water**! Let's buy the ingredients quickly so that we can have the **checker** ring **up** our order before I faint from hunger!

C. TRUE OR FALSE

1. False
2. True
3. False
4. True
5. False

6. False
7. True
8. False
9. False
10. True

D. CROSSWORD PUZZLE

R	I	P			S	L	A	S	H	E	D
I		I		V				C			
N		C	H	E	C	K	E	R			
G		K		G				A		M	
				G		B	O	T	T	O	M
				I				C		U	
		D	I	E				H		T	
				S						H	

LESSON THREE – AT THE MOVIES
LET'S WARM UP!

1. False
2. False
3. False
4. False
5. True

6. True
7. True
8. True
9. True
10. True

LET'S USE "REAL SPEAK"

A. SHOULD'A, COULD'A, WOULD'A, MUST'A

1. must'a been
2. should'a
3. must'a
4. should'a gotten

5. wouldn'a
6. could'a
7. shouldn'a
8. must'a been / wouldn'a been

LET'S PRACTICE!

A. I KNOW THE ANSWER, BUT WHAT'S THE QUESTION?

1. Did the critics enjoy the movie?
2. Were you able to get tickets for the play?
3. Do we have time to eat something before we leave?

4. Do you want to see the new musical *Felines*?
5. The movie made a fortune, didn't it?
6. Look at the long line! I thought you said this movie wasn't popular.

B. FIND YOUR PERFECT MATCH

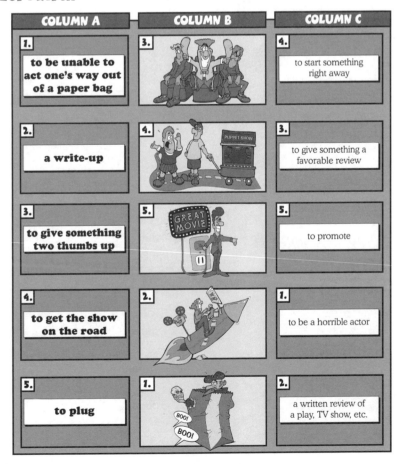

COLUMN A	COLUMN B	COLUMN C
1. to be unable to act one's way out of a paper bag	3.	4. to start something right away
2. a write-up	4. PUPPET SHOW	3. to give something a favorable review
3. to give something two thumbs up	5. GREAT MOVIE	5. to promote
4. to get the show on the road	2.	1. to be a horrible actor
5. to plug	1. BOO! BOO!	2. a written review of a play, TV show, etc.

C. IMAGINE THAT...

In this section, you could have many possible answers. Remember, respond to each situation by making a complete sentence using one of the groups of words in the word list AND using each group only once. Be as creative as you'd like!

LESSON FOUR – ON VACATION
LET'S WARM UP!

1. go to the movies
2. relax and do nothing
3. hotel with bed and breakfast
4. go swimming
5. sunbathing
6. go into town
7. completely filled
8. to accommodate us
9. take a taxicab
10. stayed awake until very late
11. visiting some interesting places
12. sleeping late

LET'S USE "REAL SPEAK"
A. PUT THE PAIRS BACK TOGETHER

1. queen
2. out
3. down
4. right
5. fork
6. pepper
7. butter
8. bad
9. jelly
10. white
11. bottom
12. cold
13. day
14. take
15. son
16. brother
17. wife
18. socks
19. ears
20. wrong
21. eggs
22. dogs

LET'S PRACTICE!

A. PRACTICE MISSING WORDS

This **B&B** has so much more charm than the hotel we stayed at last night.

a good thing they were able to **put us up** for the night. It was the only vacancy in the entire city! All the other places were booked **solid**.

We really got lucky. It's so quiet here. It was hard to **sleep** in at the other hotel because of all the noise. So, what do you want to do tonight?

Becky: Let's go hit the **town**!

Tom: Good idea. We could go **take in** a movie.

Becky: Actually, I thought it would be fun to go **sightseeing** and explore a little. We could **grab** a cab and be there in a few minutes.

Tom: After we visit the sites, we could get something to eat at that great restaurant around the corner and then go dancing till all **hours of the night**.

Becky: That's perfect! Then tomorrow we could relax all day. It would be so nice to wake up late then **hang out** by the pool and **soak up** some sun. We could even take a **dip** if it's gets too hot!

B. MATCH THE SENTENCES

1. F
2. J
3. D
4. I
5. A
6. B

7. E
8. G
9. H
10. K
11. L
12. C

LESSON FIVE – AT THE AIRPORT

LET'S WARM UP!

1. I
2. K
3. C
4. J
5. A
6. F

7. D
8. H
9. L
10. B
11. E
12. G

LET'S USE "REAL SPEAK"

A. "ACROSS" WORD PUZZLE

1. Will you go to the market to get me something to eat?
2. I have to try to find a present to give to my wife.
3. You need to know how to drive in order to buy a car.
4. If I need you to help me move tomorrow, I'll ask.
5. It's really too cold to go to the beach this morning.

B. "TA BE" OR NOT "TA BE..."

1. I went **ta** the market **ta** pick up some bread.
2. Can you tell me how **da** get **ta** the post office from here?
3. Steve wanted **da** go **da** the park but I wanted **da** go shopping instead.
4. I'd love **da** join you but I have work **ta** do.
5. On the way **da** the airport, I had **ta** stop **ta** get gas.
6. We need **da** close the windows before it starts **ta** rain.
7. I don't like **ta** go **da** the dentist.
8. Jennifer's two friends were too tired **da** go **da** the movies.

LET'S PRACTICE!

A. COMPLETE THE FAIRY TALE

Once upon a time, there was a young girl named Cinderella who lived way out in the **boonies** and wanted something fun to do. So one day, she decided to use her frequent **flyer** miles and get a free ticket to somewhere exciting. She made an appointment to sell her script to a big producer in Hollywood. She always thought that her life story would make a good movie or even a musical!

Later that day, taking only a **carry**-on, she left for the airport. She always believed in **traveling** light. Unfortunately, when she arrived at the airport, she got **bumped** because she was late. So, she was put on **standby** for the next available flight. Finally, several hours later and completely wiped **out**, she was put on the **red**-eye for Hollywood, California!

The flight was so bumpy, that she started to feel airsick and feared that she might have to use the **barf** bag. Fortunately, just then the plane made a landing in Denver. After a two-hour **layover**, she was once again on her way to Hollywood, the land of fame and fortune.

By the time she arrived, she was so **wired** that she couldn't sleep and stayed up till all **hours** of the night. Unfortunately, the combination of no sleep and jet **lag** caused her to **sleep** in late and miss her appointment with the producer!

She was so disappointed that she decided to take the next flight back home. However, as fate would have it, she found herself sitting in the airplane next to Howard, a very handsome young man, formerly known as Prince.

Cinderella and Howard, formerly known as Prince, fell in love and moved to Chicago where they lived happily ever after in a double-wide mobile home.

B. CONTEXT EXERCISE

1. K
2. E
3. F
4. C

5. G
6. A
7. D
8. I

9. B
10. J
11. L
12. H

C. COMPLETE THE PHRASE

Steve: I'm sorry we're so late. We had an unexpected two-hour **layover** some place way out in the **boonies**. You know, I almost missed the flight entirely because of all the traffic! So I arrived late and got **bumped**. Luckily they agreed to put me on **standby**. All I had was a **carry-on** so it was easy.

Karen: It's a good thing you travel **light**. Well, with the jet **lag**, I imagine you're pretty wiped **out**.

Steve: Actually, I'm pretty **wired** after all that traveling. At least I got a free ticket for being a frequent **flyer**!

Karen: So, how was it traveling on the red-**eye**?

Steve: It got a little bumpy for a while. Luckily, I never had to use the barf **bag**!

LESSON SIX – AT A RESTAURANT
LET'S WARM UP!

1. eat less
2. an additional order of
3. omit
4. pay separately
5. passion for sweets
6. You believe you can eat more than you can

7. remaining food
8. is going to be paid for by me
9. get something to eat
10. chocolate lover
11. ate in excess
12. bag to carry food home

LET'S USE "REAL SPEAK"
A. NOW YOU'RE GONNA DO A "GONNA" EXERCISE

1. I'm so hungry! I'm **gonna** pig out tonight!
2. This restaurant serves such big portions. I'm **gonna** need a doggie bag.
3. I'm starting to get fat. I'm **gonna** have to cut down on desserts.
4. I'd like a hamburger but I'm **gonna** skip the fries.
5. I'm having lunch with Irene today, but we're **gonna** go Dutch.
6. If David is anything like his mother, he's **gonna** be a chocaholic when he grows up.
7. We have a lot of extra food from the party. Steve is **gonna** take home the leftovers.
8. I'm hungry. I'm **gonna** go grab a bite.

B. IS IT GONNA OR GOING TO?

Janet and I are **going to** a great French restaurant tonight and we're **gonna** pig out! I'm probably **gonna** need a doggie bag because they serve so much food. After dinner, we're **going to** my mother's house and I'm **gonna** bring her the leftovers. In fact, I'm **gonna** order an extra chocolate dessert that I'm **gonna** surprise her with. I know that's **gonna** make her happy because she's a bigger chocaholic than I am!

LET'S PRACTICE!

A. CHOOSE THE RIGHT WORD

1. Dutch
2. doggie
3. down
4. bite
5. skip
6. tooth
7. on
8. pig
9. eyes
10. side
11. overs
12. chocolate

B. CROSSWORD PUZZLE

S	T	O	M	A	C	H	
W					H		
E					O		
E		D	U	T	C	H	
T					A		
			L		H		
B	I	T	E		O	N	
			F		L		
	C	U	T	T	I	N	G
			O		C		
			V				
S	I	D	E	R			
			R				
			S	K	I	P	
						I	
		B	A	G			

C. MATCH THE COLUMN

1. F
2. B
3. I
4. A
5. J
6. D

7. H
8. C
9. K
10. G
11. L
12. E

LET'S REVIEW! ~ THE GOOD, THE BAD, AND THE...

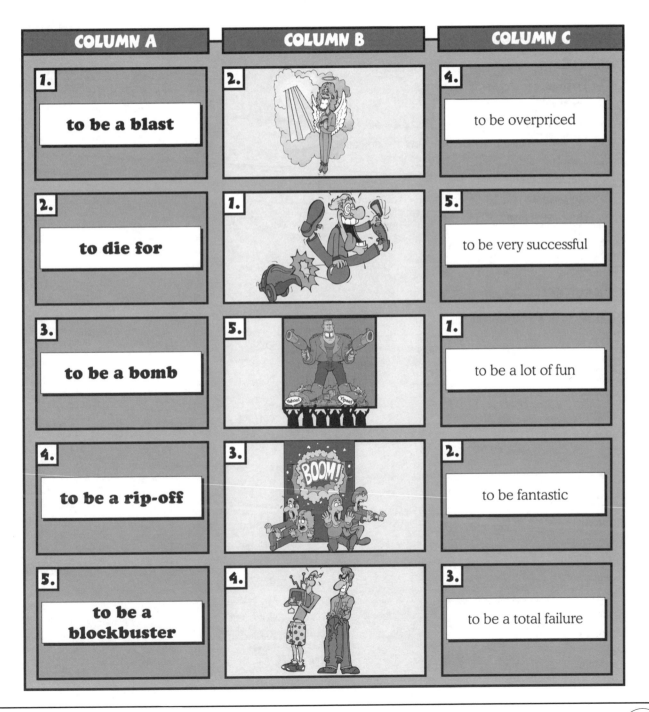

LESSON SEVEN – ON THE ROAD

LET'S WARM UP!

1. flat tire
2. destroyed
3. drove through a red light
4. drive
5. accelerate suddenly
6. minor car accident
7. the time when everyone is driving on the road
8. get in
9. arrested
10. heavy traffic
11. police officer
12. deep holes in the street
13. old car
14. tendency to drive fast

LET'S USE "REAL SPEAK"

A. WANNA OR WANSTA

1. Yes. I **wanna** see a comedy.
2. He **wansta** pig out on pizza.
3. Everybody **wansta** order hamburgers and a side of fries.
4. Yes. He **wansta** take home the leftovers in a doggie bag.
5. Yes. I **wanna** take a spin to the beach.
6. She **wansta** eat at a French restaurant.
7. Nobody **wansta** play cards tonight. Everyone **wansta** watch TV.
8. No. The cat **wansta** sleep on the sofa.

LET'S PRACTICE!

A. CORRECT OR INCORRECT

1. incorrect
2. incorrect
3. correct
4. incorrect
5. incorrect
6. correct
7. incorrect
8. incorrect
9. correct
10. correct
11. correct
12. incorrect

B. BLANK-BLANK

1. bumper-to-bumper traffic
2. go for a spin
3. ran a light
4. lead foot
5. punch it
6. fender-bender
7. hop in
8. totaled
9. clunker
10. blowout
11. cop
12. rush hour
13. pot holes
14. hauled in

C. TRUE OR FALSE

1. true
2. false
3. false
4. true
5. true

6. false
7. true
8. false
9. true
10. true

11. false
12. true
13. true
14. false

LET'S REVIEW! - IN OTHER WORDS...SYNONYMS!

1. to get on someone
2. to yank someone's chain
3. to check out
4. smash hit
5. to have a ball
6. to soak up some rays

7. way out in the boondocks
8. to pull oneself together
9. to be buzzed
10. what's the deal with...?
11. to pork out
12. to grab something

LESSON EIGHT - AT SCHOOL

LET'S WARM UP!

1. I
2. B
3. E
4. J
5. D
6. N
7. C

8. H
9. G
10. L
11. A
12. M
13. K
14. F

LET'S USE "REAL SPEAK"

A. CHANGE 'EM TO REAL SPEAK

Last night I babysat my niece and nephew. You should have seen **'em**. They're so cute! Tessa is eight years old and **'er** eyes look just like **'er** mother's. When you look at **'em** in the sunlight, they look very dark blue. **Her** favorite food is ice cream and **'er** favorite color is red. **Her** brother Nicholas just had **'is** fifth birthday. Everyone thinks **'e** looks just like **'is** father but **'e** thinks **'e** looks like **'is** grandfather. Frankly, whenever I see **'im** smile, I think **'e** looks just like me! After all, I'm **'is** uncle! Both of **'em** love to read. Yesterday, Tessa read a story to **'er** mother and Nicholas read one to **'is** father. I'm glad they live so close. It's so much fun watching **'em** grow up!

LET'S PRACTICE!

A. TRUTH OR LIE

1. lie
2. lie
3. lie

4. truth
5. truth
6. truth

B. FIND THE DEFINITION

1. to do extremely well on a test
2. to do extremely poorly on a test
3. to study very hard in a short period of time
4. to miss class intentionally
5. to remove a class from one's schedule
6. an end-of-term test which covers everything learned during the school term
7. extremely difficult or terrific
8. a test that can be taken again at a later time
9. a surprise test
10. a common abbreviation for "psychology"
11. to stay up all night studying
12. perfect grades

C.

FIND-THE-WORD GRID

```
T N W U F S (A C E D) G R R E W D W T M A T
H O H T O E G R O A O O E D H S E O E M A
V W Y L R V O S U T D S D R I M L G L F R
Y T (S T R A I G H T) I E A O C E L O U L V
E H O W K N U R T N P S N P O P I H N U E
I I T O O Y R O H U L A D E R S T A C N T
Q I T X R E F U C N E R V B E Y S V H K O
U C R (K I L L E R) D D E I L M C T E O T D
E U Y W N R T H A E G R (N I G H T E R) O E
I T T W D S H T M R E E L E N N M O I S A
```

LET'S REVIEW! - A FUN TIME WAS HAD BY ALL

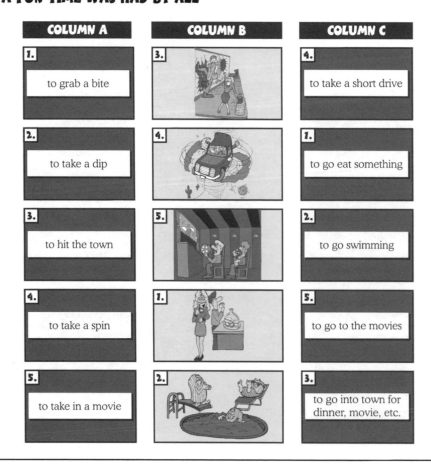

COLUMN A	COLUMN B	COLUMN C
1. to grab a bite	**3.**	**4.** to take a short drive
2. to take a dip	**4.**	**1.** to go eat something
3. to hit the town	**5.**	**2.** to go swimming
4. to take a spin	**1.**	**5.** to go to the movies
5. to take in a movie	**2.**	**3.** to go into town for dinner, movie, etc.

LESSON NINE – TO YOUR HEALTH

LET'S WARM UP!

1. feverish
2. recover
3. fainted
4. feeling very sick
5. in good health
6. very bored
7. relax
8. become very restless from confinement
9. full of energy
10. nervous and agitated
11. survive
12. ill
13. lose strength on its own
14. tired and lifeless

LET'S USE "REAL SPEAK"

A. UNSCRAMBLE

1. What did you get for your birthday?
   What did **ya** get for **yer** birthday?
2. Are you going to your mother's house?
   Are **ya** going to **yer** mother's house?
3. You gave all your money to your brother?
   Ya gave all **yer** money to **yer** brother?
4. You know you are my best friend.
   Ya know **yer** my best friend.
5. Are you going to get your car washed today?
   Are **ya** going to get **yer** car washed today?

LET'S PRACTICE!

A. THE UNFINISHED CONVERSATION

In this exercise, be as creative as you'd like. Make sure to use the slang and idioms provided.

B. CHOOSE THE RIGHT WORD

1. under
2. crazy
3. running
4. dog
5. pull
6. mind
7. run
8. pink
9. blah
10. back
11. out
12. antsy
13. easy
14. go

C. COMPLETE THE STORY

Today I went to visit my grandmother but she was _under the weather_.

She said that she was feeling kind of _blah_ this morning and then by the afternoon,

she was _running a fever_. She'll _pull through_

just fine but for now, she's _bored out of her mind_. I suppose I'd go

stir crazy too if I were _as sick as a dog_ and

couldn't leave the house. She'll _bounce back_ and be

raring to go in just a few days. When you catch a cold or a flu, you just have to let it

run its course. The most important thing is that you

need to _take it easy_ and get plenty of rest and drink plenty of

liquids. Then you'll be back _in the pink_ in no time!

LET'S REVIEW! - THE NIGHT SHIFT

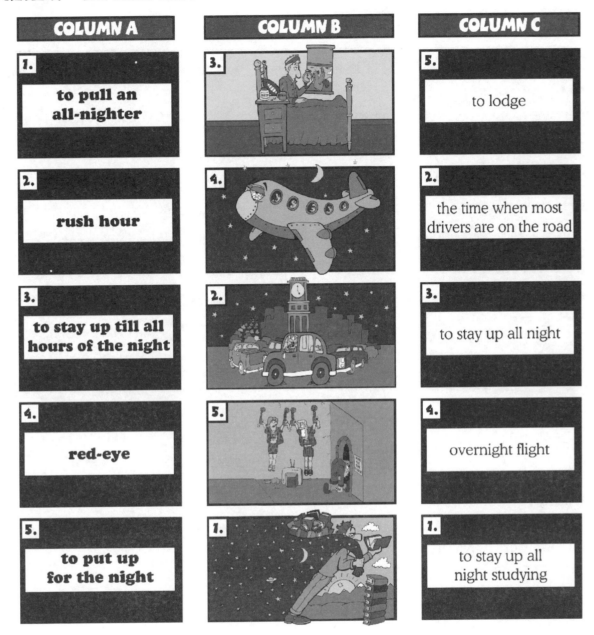

COLUMN A	COLUMN B	COLUMN C
1. to pull an all-nighter	**3.**	**5.** to lodge
2. rush hour	**4.**	**2.** the time when most drivers are on the road
3. to stay up till all hours of the night	**2.**	**3.** to stay up all night
4. red-eye	**5.**	**4.** overnight flight
5. to put up for the night	**1.**	**1.** to stay up all night studying

LESSON TEN - ON A DATE

LET'S WARM UP!

1. True
2. False
3. True
4. True
5. True
6. False
7. True
8. True
9. False
10. True
11. True
12. True
13. True
14. True
15. False

LET'S USE "REAL SPEAK"

A. NOW YOU HAFTA DO A "HAFTA" EXERCISE

> # THE ABSOLUTE BEST CHOCOLATE SOUFFLÉ RECIPE IN THE WORLD
>
> When making a chocolate soufflé, you **hafta** start with fresh ingredients. The eggs **hafta** be room temperature and the chocolate **hasta** be the dark or bittersweet kind. Believe it or not, all you **hafta** buy at the store is two large packages of chocolate chips, eight eggs, and a cup of whipping cream. All you **hafta** do is heat up the cream and pour it over the chocolate chips and stir until it's all combined. The cream **hasta** be hot enough to melt the chocolate but make sure the cream doesn't boil! Beat the eggs in a bowl and add the chocolate mixture, continuing to beat until it's all nice and creamy. You don't even **hafta** separate the eggs for this soufflé, which makes it really easy! Pour the mixture into a soufflé bowl and carefully put it in a pre-heated 350-degree oven. The soufflé **hasta** cook for one hour....and POOF! You'll have the lightest and most chocolaty soufflé you've ever tasted!

LET'S PRACTICE!

A. & B. CREATE YOUR OWN STORY (PARTS 1 & 2)

Create your own word list. Be as creative as you can!

C. WHAT WOULD YOU DO IF SOMEONE SAID...

1. b
2. a
3. c
4. b
5. b

6. c
7. c
8. a
9. b
10. b

LET'S REVIEW! - SOME OPPOSITES DO ATTRACT!

1. D
2. E
3. B

4. C
5. A

INDEX

NOTES TO REMEMBER

1.
2.
3.
4.
5.
6.
7.
8.
9.
10.
11.
12.
13.
14.
15.
16.
17.
18.
19.
20.
21.
22.
23.
24.
25.
26.
27.
28.
29.

NOTES TO REMEMBER

1.
2.
3.
4.
5.
6.
7.
8.
9.
10.
11.
12.
13.
14.
15.
16.
17.
18.
19.
20.
21.
22.
23.
24.
25.
26.
27.
28.
29.

NOTES TO REMEMBER

1.
2.
3.
4.
5.
6.
7.
8.
9.
10.
11.
12.
13.
14.
15.
16.
17.
18.
19.
20.
21.
22.
23.
24.
25.
26.
27.
28.
29.

NOTES TO REMEMBER

1.
2.
3.
4.
5.
6.
7.
8.
9.
10.
11.
12.
13.
14.
15.
16.
17.
18.
19.
20.
21.
22.
23.
24.
25.
26.
27.
28.
29.

NOTES TO REMEMBER

1.
2.
3.
4.
5.
6.
7.
8.
9.
10.
11.
12.
13.
14.
15.
16.
17.
18.
19.
20.
21.
22.
23.
24.
25.
26.
27.
28.
29.

SLANGMAN® PUBLISHING

*"If you don't know slang & idioms, you don't know the **REAL** language!"*

ALL THE BOOKS IN THE SERIES INCLUDE...

- ☐ Dialogues using popular slang & idioms
- ☐ Context exercises
- ☐ Column matching
- ☐ Find-the-slang-word drills
- ☐ Hundreds of illustrations
- ☐ Vocabulary drills and games
- ☐ Fill-in exercises
- ☐ Matching the picture with the idiom
- ☐ Reading, writing, listening, & speaking exercises
- ☐ Crossword puzzles
- ***...plus you can use the books in any order!***

STREET SPEAK 1
THE COMPLETE COURSE IN AMERICAN SLANG & IDIOMS

Includes slang, idioms, and jargon associated with:
- ☐ Parties
- ☐ The Airport
- ☐ The Market
- ☐ Dating
- ☐ Movies
- ☐ Vacations
- ☐ Restaurants
- ☐ Your Health

Book: 144 pages **ISBN: 1891888-080 • US $22.95**

BIZ SPEAK 1
SLANG, IDIOMS & JARGON USED IN BUSINESS ENGLISH

Includes slang, idioms, and jargon associated with
- ☐ The Workplace
- ☐ Negotiations
- ☐ Computers
- ☐ The Internet / E-Commerce
- ☐ Acronyms and Shortcu
- ☐ Meetings
- ☐ Abbreviations
- ☐ Marketing and Advertisi

Book: 230 pages **ISBN: 1891888-145 • US $24.95**

STREET SPEAK 2
THE COMPLETE COURSE IN AMERICAN SLANG & IDIOMS

Includes slang, idioms, and jargon associated with:
- ☐ Houseguests
- ☐ Shopping
- ☐ Subway
- ☐ Birthdays
- ☐ Workplace
- ☐ Babysitting
- ☐ Telephone
- ☐ Aches & Pains

Book: 232 pages **ISBN: 1891888-064 • US $24.95**

BIZ SPEAK 2
SLANG, IDIOMS & JARGON USED IN BUSINESS ENGLISH

Includes slang, idioms, and jargon associated with:
- ☐ The Workplace
- ☐ International Trade
- ☐ Business Tra
- ☐ Sports terms used in business
- ☐ Shipping
- ☐ Globaliza
- ☐ "Bureaucratese"
- ☐ and more!

Book: 230 pages **ISBN: 1891888-153 • US $24.95**

Now ***hear*** how Americans really speak! Audio CDs and Mp3s conta
all the dialogues from the books, plus all the vocabulary lessons a

STREET SPEAK 3
THE COMPLETE COURSE IN AMERICAN SLANG & IDIOMS

Includes slang, idioms, and jargon associated with:
- ☐ Dating/Relationships
- ☐ TV & Movies
- ☐ Sports
- ☐ Emergencies
- ☐ Political Correctness
- ☐ Teens
- ☐ plus Foreign Words Used by Everyone
- ☐ Alliterations, Repeating Words, & Proverbs

Book: 240 pages **ISBN: 1891888-226 • US $24.95**

Preview the chapters and order online!
WWW.SLANGMAN.COM

Fax: 413-647-1589
Email: info@slangman.com • Website: www.slangman.c

SLANGMAN KIDS
Foreign Language Through Fairy Tales

ages 3+

Each fairy tale starts in English, then "morphs" into the language being taught!

Chinese - French - German - Hebrew - Italian - Japanese - Spanish

It's fun! It's fast! It's really easy!

Kids learn foreign languages quickly by reading (and listening to) their favorite fairy tales that start in English, but slowly turn into the language they're learning! By the end of each story, kids quickly learn 20+ new foreign language words. Each level introduces 20 MORE words and *includes words learned in the previous levels!* By the end of the series, the fairy tales will be written almost entirely in the foreign language! *(Available in foreign language-to-English versions, too!)*

Preview the chapters and order online!
WWW.SLANGMAN.COM
Fax: 413-647-1589
Email: info@slangman.com • Website: www.slangman.com